ISBN: 978-1-942810-17-9

MASTERING AMAZON DESCRIPTIONS

AN AUTHOR'S GUIDE

BRIAN D. MEEKS

CONTENTS

CHAPTER ONE

WHAT'S THE GOAL?

It's to make you enjoy copywriting.

This may seem insane because most authors I know hate writing their descriptions more than they hate street mimes beating baby seals with giant blocks of frozen veal. I used to feel that way, too. But here's the thing: it can change your life.

I'm talking about giving you the chance to convert at up to three times what you're doing now. I've seen it with many authors. Your book probably requires 30 clicks to get a conversion, which is a sale or a KU download for those who are exclusive. That's what my descriptions needed before I found copywriting. Now they only need 8 to 10.

Are you ready to start?

Will you take this seriously enough that you aim to become a quality copywriter and not just barely good enough to improve your current debacle of a description?

I hope the first two answers were "yes," but if they weren't, maybe it's because you need proof. Perhaps a demonstration of the power of copywriting would be in order?

We're less than 200 words into this book, and I've got a little homework for you. It's in two parts, and I hope it will do three things:

- Demonstrate the power of copywriting and proper copywriting formatting.
- Convince you to make copywriting part of your daily life. I mean, when you're done, I hope you'll use the techniques taught

here in every bit of non-prose writing you create. I mean every
newsletter, email correspondence, and most importantly, every
single Facebook post you write.
- Lastly, make me piles of money.

Convincing the Skeptic

Step 1: I need you to look at your Facebook posts. I mean the ones
you've posted, whether it's a share or an original post, you just need click on
your name, next to the "Home" button at the top of Facebook and check
them out. Maybe skip one if it's less than an hour old, but then write down
the number of comments and "likes or loves or ha ha ha," etc.

So, you should have two columns, the first is comments, the second we'll
call "likes" and then to the left, one through ten.

No.	Comments	Likes
1.	19	63
2.	37	46
3.	71	108
4.	35	67
5.	15	55
6.	13	46
7.	17	223
8.	14	46
9.	10	48
10.	20	54

This is what my feed looks like. I have 3,158 friends. And they are vastly
more active on my posts since I started using copywriting all the time. I used
to get around 5 comments and 10 likes.

Please take the time to do this, because when you finish the book and
start practicing copywriting on everything, it's going to blow your mind how
the power of words can get a reaction.

Step 2: (Warning: This step has the potential to financially help the author a
bunch, but it will demonstrate the power of copywriting.)

I want you to copy an ad I'm going to write for *Mastering Amazon
Descriptions: An Author's Guide.*

Most authors have at least a few Facebook friends who are authors, so this post will make sense to them. And if it works, it has the potential to sell lots of books. Plus, if your friends on Facebook learn proper copywriting and you've all read my book, you'll be able to help each other out. The easiest way to learn copywriting for descriptions is to work on someone else's description when they ask.

IMPORTANT: Retype it as it appears here below, between the asterisks, with the blank lines. The blank lines are crucial to making the copy seem non-threatening, meaning not a giant block of text. To get blank lines on Facebook, hold down <shift> and hit <enter> twice.

Post this on Facebook:

It's finally here…

…the book on description-writing Brian Meeks promised last year.

I've always hated writing descriptions. But if it helps get more sales and downloads with fewer paid clicks, then I'm going to devour every word. And then, I'll likely read it again.

If you've read his books before, you'll know Brian is pretty snarky. I like his humor, and he makes subjects I dread, fun.

I can't wait to get started.

Here's a link: books2read.com/u/38xZx7

Check it out.

———

Note: If you're reading a print book, you'll probably need to type the link into a browser, then copy and paste that result into Facebook. And for those reading on Kindle, probably the same thing unless you're using the desktop version of Kindle Reader, then you could just click the link and copy and paste. Yes, it's a pain, but the exercise will be enlightening.

———

Step 3: Watch the reaction, reply to any comments you get, and see the power of copywriting. If you are put off by the idea of me trying to sell my book, then don't do it.

Analysis: So what's going on here?

I started with a hook. It's short, and because I didn't say what "it" was, people are naturally going to move on to the next line. That's the first goal of copywriting, according to legendary copywriter Joseph Sugarman.

Then I put in a bit that is true for 99% of authors. Everyone hates writing descriptions, and if you can strike a nerve, they will continue to read. Next, I addressed an objection people have to reading about a subject that they hate: "Will it be dry?"

If you've read *Mastering Amazon Ads: An Author's Guide*, then you know it will be an enjoyable read.

Lastly, I finish with a call-to-action. They are so ubiquitous that we don't even notice them—but they work. Madison Avenue proved that in the fifties, and ads have been asking us to buy ever since.

Some people hate them, so, if you're one of those, then don't use it. You'll get fewer sales, but that's okay. You'll feel good about being such a rebel. (I'm kidding... USE A CTA ALWAYS... I don't care if you hate them.)

That's your first bit of homework.

Do it now, and then keep reading. This book is not only going to show you how to write descriptions (there are a bunch from all sorts of different genres and some non-fiction, too), but you'll see examples of articles I've written on various subjects that are important for authors. Each of these was written with proper copywriting.

And if you're a member of the 20BooksTo50K group, you can still find many of these pinned to the All-Star thread. Go look one or two up and check out the numbers of likes and comments. I have gotten as many as 750 people to like and several hundred to comment on posts that are up to 1,500 words long.

Do you know how hard it is to get people to read that long a post?

It's impossible without copywriting, but I manage it.

It's time to get to work.

Let's do this!

CHAPTER TWO

You won't believe this story...

There was a woman. She was like many women her age. She had kids, a husband, and a social circle that involved dance recitals and soccer games. Then one day, she got an idea.

She thought it just might make her perfect life even better.

The voice in her head objected. It told her she was dumb. It suggested that dreaming was a bad idea and would only lead to disappointment. This woman—we shall call her GP—always listened to the voice. Even when she thought it might be wrong.

Three weeks after she had the wonderful idea that the little voice talked her out of, she had another thought. This time, she kept it to herself so the little voice wouldn't be mean. And it worked. There was nary a peep.

GP fed the ideas with questions that started with "What if," and before she knew it, she had more than an idea, more than a dream—she had a story.

It was a good story.

So, she wrote it down.

GP started to put in hours and hours researching everything there was to know about self-publishing. She was going to put her novel up on Amazon, and then she was going to write another. She didn't care what anyone, least of all her little voice (who had found out what GP was up to), said.

It was fun.

It turns out dreaming wasn't such a dangerous thing after all.

There were tons of stories of people just like her writing many books and finding readers. If they could do it, she could, too. She had a vivid imagination. GP even once pictured a scene where her husband went to the grocery store and returned with the item she'd asked him to get.

Of course, that never really happened, but she could imagine it coming true. That was the point. If she could imagine it, she could write it.

One day, while sitting on a bench outside of her daughter's dance class, a strange little elf-like creature sat down next to her. His name was Wiggington. He was evil, but she didn't know that. A fanciful name can fool most.

Wiggington asked if she knew the difference between the words causation and correlation.

It seemed like an odd question, but Mr. Wiggington was wearing a bowler hat, so she felt compelled to answer. "No, I do not."

He smiled at her and tipped his hat. He said nothing more as he started reading his copy of the London Times.

This struck GP as odd because she lived in a small mid-western town in America. Where does one get a London Times around here, she thought?

It didn't matter, so she went back to reading the bodice-ripper she had on her Kindle app.

Two weeks passed. She hit publish on her first novel. It was an exciting moment. Her husband said he was extra proud of her and washed and put away the dishes (albeit in the wrong spots). Then he got the kids to bed and let GP have some quiet time—a rarity in her house.

But she couldn't be quiet. She wanted to check her numbers. GP wanted to sell books.

When she finally went to bed, there had been two sales, and she felt amazing. To think that two people she didn't know were reading her book was thrilling. But when she awoke the next morning, the worst thing in the world happened.

No, her husband hadn't tried to make breakfast.

She looked, and there hadn't been any more sales.

All those hours she slept and with billions of people still awake in the world, and none of them had given her book a try. Was it her author picture? She'd never liked her hair in that one. Had they "looked inside" and decided it was rubbish?

A million things ran through her mind. GP was panicked.

She fed the children (which for the sake of this story included Mr. GP. He had eggs and bacon and said it was delicious.)

As soon as the pack was sent out the door to the job and school, she got to work. A quick look at Facebook confirmed the world hadn't ended, and she was off to the forums. Loads of other authors were talking about book stuff, and it got overwhelming.

It was clear she still had a lot to learn.

Writing time went well. She put on her favorite Baroque music and shut off all the browsers in her head. GP was good at getting into the zone. In two hours, she had written 2037 words and introduced a new character. His name was Brad, and he was handsome, smart, and kind to animals. Was he also possibly a serial killer? Yes, but he was REALLY handsome, and she figured everyone has faults. She liked Brad.

When school ended, it was time to take the kids to soccer practice. There was the usual chatter among the mom set.

When everyone tired and went back to their phones, she noticed the elf in the bowler hat was sitting in a lawn chair rooting for his son, who seemed to be the goalie for the team wearing the red practice jerseys. Why hadn't she noticed an elven goalie before?

GP went over and said, "Hello. Are you enjoying the practice?"

"Oh, yes. I enjoy footie at all levels," he said pointing to the Dortmund bag by his chair. "They're fourth in the Bundesliga right now."

GP nodded. She didn't know what he was talking about, but he seemed excited.

He offered her the lawn chair next to him.

Had that been there when she walked up?

It didn't matter. GP sat down, and they cheered as his boy made a diving save.

"How are you doing today, on a scale of 1 to 37?" he asked.

GP thought about it, and the memories of her morning and afternoon resulting in zero sales made her sad. She said, "Oh, maybe a twenty."

"That's a wee bit low," he said sounding more like a leprechaun than an elf.

"I wrote a book. Zero sales today."

"You're an author?" he exclaimed with no small measure of being impressed.

"It's just one book. I wouldn't call myself an author."

"That's interesting. How many books does one need to author to be an author?"

GP didn't have an answer.

"May I make a suggestion?"

"Sure."

The elf looked at her with his piercing black eyes and said, "Find out who the top sellers in your genre are and do what they do. Copy their descriptions and copy their style of back matter. If they're selling so many books, it must be right."

GP thanked him.

She didn't know that he was evil.

She didn't understand correlation and causation.

It seemed reasonable, and so that's just what she did—with mediocre results. For years to come, she struggled without ever knowing why.

And the evil elf in the bowler hat laughed and laughed and laughed. Sometimes he kicked puppies, but mostly he laughed and laughed and laughed.

———

I'd like to answer the question on every single reader's mind.

And I'm pretty sure I've got this correct:

"WTF?"

Admittedly, I, too, am laughing.

The point to this story is that most of you are NOT data geeks. You don't know the difference between correlation and causation. You may not know the difference between an increase of twenty percent or twenty points.

They are little things.

Yet they are as common a thing to know for data analysts as knowing how to deal with a teething toddler is to mothers. I'm not a parent, so I have no idea how much brandy you're supposed to give children to get them to stop crying. I would have to Google it.

The point is, there's an answer to all these questions.

Now I might be wrong in guessing half a bottle of brandy, but I'm not wrong in saying that "Do as the successful people are doing" may be a horrible idea.

Did that person making $1,000,000 per year ever analyze their description's results?

If you were making $1,000,000 per year, would you question it?

The answer to both questions, as far as my talking with authors who make a million dollars per year (and there's more of them than you might guess), is no.

This then begs the question, why follow the lead of someone who is just guessing?

And, more importantly, how many millions of dollars did they leave on the table by not doing "the math?" And now I'll answer your second question—one which I'm sure has just occurred to most of you and may have a few curled up in the fetal position: "In this book I've just shelled out my hard-earned money for, which is supposed to be about copywriting, will there be math?"

Yes!

And it's the fun kind of math.

In fact, the math is the best part of the book. Don't worry, though; if *Mastering Amazon Ads: An Author's Guide*, didn't kill you then this book will be a breeze.

Are you ready to get started?

CHAPTER THREE

OKAY, THE FACT THAT YOU'RE HERE, IN CHAPTER 3, MEANS YOU'VE earned twenty points.

You also earned ten points just for buying the book. Writing descriptions is awful. You hate it. I used to hate it. Some have called the need to write descriptions a war crime. Why can't the readers just judge my book by its awesome cover?

Well, they can't.

I know of what I speak. For I, too, hated writing descriptions before I heard a chorus of angels tell me that learning copywriting was the way forward. (Note: It might have been that I was listening to a Slovenian choir do their version of Africa by Toto on YouTube, but the point is the same... I saw the light.)

I once put off launching a book for six weeks because of the description. Every day, I would say to myself, "Okay, just bang out a three-hundred-word synopsis and be done with it." Then I would eat bacon, play a video game, and take a nap. Admittedly, it was a GREAT six weeks.

When I finally put up the synopsis, it was horrible. But I didn't care. It was done.

A year later, I decided to do the unthinkable. I would learn copywriting. I expected it would be like eating peas, or going to the DMV (twice), or dying by bear mauling after an ill-advised woodland cuddle attempt. It turns out, it was sort of awesome.

But I didn't know that right away.

It wasn't until I saw the data that I was, in the words of a teenager, "Totally, like, you know, totally... you know... happy."

Once I saw my new conversion rate, I went back and estimated how much money I'd left on the table. I looked at the twelve months prior. I had all the clicks. I knew what "would have" happened if I had made the change then, and the number was staggering. In twelve months, I would have earned an additional $60,000 in revenue with proper copywriting.

I told this story in my other book. And I'll say it again: "Don't cry for me Argentina." I'm an optimist, and when I saw that number my first thought was, Whew! I'm glad I didn't wait another year.

You see, mindset is important.

There's an old adage that goes, "Don't cry over spilled vodka." I think it was said by a Russian man who actually had another bottle in the cupboard and one hidden in the barn for good measure. So we don't know if he would have cried at spilling his last bottle. I digress.

The calendar is your extra bottles of vodka. Go ahead, turn the page. There's another month just waiting for you. It's better to look forward to that month and the extra sales than to spend time going back to the old months and lamenting opportunity lost.

Throw out the old calendar, unless it has pictures of guinea pigs competing in Olympic-style events. Guinea pigs are adorable.

Where was I?

Mindset.

You're going to need to think differently about your book.

This will be the hardest thing to change when you first start writing your descriptions. You'll want to write a synopsis. You'll want to tell the potential reader all the yummy goodness contained within the pages.

Don't do it.

Why buy the book if you already told them what happens?

"But Brian, that's what everybody does. They can't all be wrong, can they?"

Yes, they can.

The numbers don't lie.

When I first started to change out my descriptions, they were converting at 1:30 (reads one-in-thirty). That means that 29 people were NOT buying my book. When I made the change, it dropped immediately to 1:10 – 1:12.

It should be noted that when I was making these changes, I was getting a high volume of clicks per day, so the results were easy to see.

If you're not getting too many clicks through your advertising venue of choice, then it may take a while to have enough data to see the results.

This brings me to my first **WARNING:**

WARNING: DO NOT CHANGE YOUR DESCRIPTION,
LOOK AT THE NEXT DAY'S SALES, SEE THEY'VE DROPPED
(WHICH COULD HAPPEN FOR A NUMBER OF REASONS
UNRELATED TO THE DESCRIPTION), AND PANIC.

DO **NOT** PANIC.

"But how could the sales drop if the new description is so good? Are you messing with me?"

No, I'm not.

If your books don't sell in great numbers from one day to the next, then it's important to understand how much variance you have for your book. Look at the sales over the previous 90 days. Calculate a 15-day moving average. Note the high days and low days. Were there any promotions?

Don't worry—I'm going to explain what all of those things mean and how to use them.

This is **IMPORTANT**. You need to do the math, both before and after the change. This is NOT something you can eyeball, and you may not get it right on your first try... but you might.

I don't want you to give up on a description too early. Variance can be a cruel mistress.

This may seem like I'm beating a deceased equine, but I need to convince you that all of this math stuff matters.

Some of the "number of reasons" there might be a drop in sales include:

1. The day before, you randomly had a spike due to organic traffic.
2. Variance is real.
3. Poltergeists.

Okay, the last one may be tough for me to prove, but let's take a look at variance.

Variance can cause data to look better than it is or worse than reality. It works both ways. I have a perfect example.

Before I learned copywriting, my books converted at 1:30 with one at 1:35. On one of the books, I had an ad that only got 5 clicks. The AMS report told me there were 5 sales. (If you know me, you'll know I rail against the inaccuracy of the AMS report and that it is NEVER to be believed, but I've not found any instances where it over-reported. Thus, I believe the five sales.)

Now, if you do the math, it should take 150 clicks to get 5 sales. Of course, that's based upon a 1:30 number that is made up of many thousands of clicks to analyze. In a short period, like the example, with five clicks, it is mathematically possible to get five readers in a row who want to buy the book.

It is also possible to go zero for one hundred or worse.

I'm sure that if the ad had continued to run, there would have been many more clicks without sales, so the 1:1 conversion rate would have plummeted.

The important point is that it happened and that it's really unlikely.

How unlikely?

2.5 million to one against a one-in-thirty proposition coming in five times in a row. Yes, I live in Las Vegas and may have busted out some gambler talk. The important thing is that I'll need another 2.5 million ads to realistically have a shot at going 5 for 5 again. And even then, because of variance, it could be 5 million. I could look at the ads of every author I know, for the next hundred years, and still never see 5 for 5.

And yet it happened.

If you don't have a lot of data, you can't draw conclusions.

CHAPTER FOUR

WHY ARE ALL THE DESCRIPTIONS WRONG?

Before I get into that, let me say that I imagine the way descriptions are done now may have been effective in the past. I don't know.

What I do know is we live in the age of social media. Time is short. We have kitty pictures to like, guinea pigs eating vegetable videos to watch, and hate-filled rants about people who don't agree with us politically to write. It takes time. So we can't be bothered to read massive paragraphs outlining a book that we intend to sit down with and enjoy, uninterrupted, for hours on end.

Yes, the irony is strong in this logic.

This means your book, the one you love more than your first two children (the third one turned out okay), must capture the potential reader's attention in less time than it takes to check out the shoes of the offensively pretty woman at the party and judge her.

You need a hook.

What's a hook?

They are everywhere. In commercials, on billboards, and especially on those links that pretend to be articles at the bottom of your most trusted online fake news site. "You won't believe how she looks today?" with a picture of an actress from Friends.

You know it's clickbait.

You also know that the actress pictured won't be shown until page 34... if at all.

The chances of being pissed off are greater than 98%.

…and yet you click.

That's a hook.

You're the fish who knew the worm was plastic, but you just couldn't resist. And now you've arrived at the website. If enough people get hooked, some of them will click on one of the ads for something else that they don't need.

And that's how Viagra gets sold in droves.

Wouldn't you like your books to sell like that?

I'm getting excited just thinking about it.

Do you know what is NOT a hook?

A story about a boy who did this thing and then met this girl and they did another thing. Then they went on an adventure. They did three more things.

If you like a book about people doing the things listed above, you'll like, The Boy Who Did the Thing.

Yes, that's how your description reads right now.

This is where I begin with all the descriptions I write. Imagine a person has just clicked on a link that took them to your book's description. There are only a few lines "above the fold." Their eyes will scan that tiny white space quickly to find the "read more" and click it.

Now because we know it's been several seconds since they've checked their Facebook feed to see if the post about their freshly mowed lawn has received any more likes, and they're getting the shakes and need to get back to those wonderful "external validation" dopamine hits, you've got much less time to hook them than it takes to read this dreadfully long sentence.

If your first paragraph is long like the one above, you've lost the battle.

In fact, if there are any paragraphs as long as that one, you've lost some of them.

The three nanosecond scan of the entire description is followed by the voice in the reader's head either saying, "okay" or "I can't be bothered."

It's worth mentioning again.

People scan and judge.

Intimidating blocks of text without hooks won't get them to read.

So, what does that mean?

You need to start small catch their attention.

My rule of thumb is to try to craft a short hook that is six words or fewer. Given a choice between the character's name, Alexandra McExtraordinairlyLongName or the pronoun "she," choose the latter.

Short is good.

This is the first thing about description copywriting you need to remember.

Write short hooks!

Homework: Write 5 hooks for your favorite book. Each one must be less than six words.

CHAPTER FIVE

Don't tell or show...
...hint.

Imagine you've read chapter four. I'm guessing since we're in chapter five, that won't be a stretch. Now let's say you did the homework, and because it caused you a lot of stress, you are now drinking wine.

This is a good time to talk about an important idea.

Are you ready?

Okay. I'll wait while you open another bottle.

Good. Now let's begin.

Don't tell them what happens in the book. Instead, hint at what might happen. In nearly every description I help an author with, they have perfectly good hints hidden in their statements of fact about the plot.

John will save his family from a horrible death and torture at the hands of rogue, door-to-door cleaning supply salesmen.

No. This is bad.

Can John save his family from a fate worse than death?

Yes. This is copywriting.

In the first version, it's just a spoiler. Why read the book? We know what's going to happen and that the hero will win.

Now we probably know the hero is going to win anyway, but if you don't tell them that, it makes for a more interesting read. And if you've ever enjoyed any of the dead Russian authors, you know that a happy conclusion is NOT assured. I love Ivan Turgenev.

What about the second version?

There are two hooks. The first one is obvious: will the protagonist, John, save his family? The second one is, "What is a fate worse than death?"

That makes me want to read more.

To be clear, I don't mean to say that it makes me want to read more of the book. It makes me want to read the next line of the description.

This is the major theme from the wonderful book, The Adweek Copywriting Handbook: The Ultimate Guide to Writing Powerful Advertising and Marketing Copy from One of America's Top Copywriters, by Joseph Sugarman.

I do wonder if the horrible title (bad copywriting) is meant to be ironic. I mean, I had to take a nap after the word "writing" to have the energy to read all the way to the end of the title. That can't be good for sale conversions.

It should also be noted that the description for the Sugarman book is dreadful with a capital D (and all the other letters, too).

But it's still a great book.

This is the book that put me on the path. His main theme is that a copywriter's job is to hook the reader enough to get them to read the next line.

And that line should focus all its efforts on getting them to read the one after that.

This should continue until suddenly, the potential customer is at the end of the ad and only needs the tiniest nudge to get them to buy.

"Get it now."

Does this make sense?

Go read one of your descriptions. Is there a point where you feel fatigued? Well, probably not. You love this book more than your first two children.

That wasn't a good example. My bad.

Instead, go read the description of any of the versions of the worst writer in American history, Ernest Hemingway's A Farewell to Arms. Yes, the book that Bradley Cooper threw out the window and nearly lost his mind over in the wonderfully moving Silver Linings Playbook.

I'm being serious. Stop reading my book. Put down the wine. Go to Amazon and read it now.

It's a good thing you've been drinking because if you had tried that sober, it might have been life-threatening. Such boring descriptions. The first time I read a description for a Hemingway book, I was hospitalized for over 200 years. They had to put me into stasis to keep me alive.

Still, it's less painful than reading A Farewell to Arms. I read it in a previous life and died immediately... twice.

How many potential readers have you killed?
So, what have we learned thus far?

1. Hooks are important.
2. Hint at what might happen. Don't tell (or show) what will happen.
3. Just because a successful person has a description that is a giant block of text, it does NOT mean that's the way to do it... unless you're a cold-hearted murdering bastard. Then, by all means, write a terrible description.

Bonus: A copywriting experiment.

This will be fun.

1. Go to Facebook and find a post you feel deserves a comment.
2. Write a response using proper copywriting.
3. This means an opening hook of six words or less. Then, by holding down <shift>, you'll hit <enter> twice to add a blank line.
4. Now write a bit more but keep it hooky.
5. Another blank line.
6. Then finish with a question. (This represents your CTA.)
7. Compare how many likes and comments you get to your normal comments on people's posts.

This is how I respond to all Facebook posts. I only write like a copy-writer. It's amazing practice. The results are clear that it keeps people reading and improves the likelihood of a conversion, which in this case is a comment in reply to your comment.
Good luck.

CHAPTER SIX

Why is practice is important?

An example of hubris:

By now, I'm assuming your significant other has put the children to bed after answering the obvious question as to why you're laughing so much and what's with all the empty bottles.

"It's a funny book, and recycling is important," is the answer that puts their minds to rest.

Copywriting takes practice.

The initial results can lead one (in this case, me) to conclude erroneously that the first attempt is pure gold. It's likely only copper at best.

The problem with huge gains in conversion rate is that the numbers can be dazzling. This can lead to a feeling of genius. I was so pleased at driving my conversion rates from 1:30 to 1:10 that I assumed I had written the perfect description.

It could not be better.

This was the last description I'd ever need to write for that book because I was so clever to nail it the first try.

I was not clever.

And I lived with a description that could be improved for over a year and a half. It was pure hubris.

I started to work with authors on their descriptions. This came from my Mastering Amazon Ads: An Author's Guide beta group on Facebook. People would reach out to me and ask for help. I like helping, so I'd take a crack at their description.

Here's an important point:

I hadn't read their books. All I knew about the story was what I gathered from their original description, which was generally a spoiler-filled synopsis. This made it easier for me to craft hooks and hints at the story than it was for the authors.

It took a long time for me to get good enough at being detached to take another crack at my own books. It will take you a while, too. That's why the Bonus Exercise from the last chapter is so important. It will make you a quality copywriter more quickly.

Again, you'll struggle with your descriptions more than if you tried writing a hook-filled description for an author friend.

If you keep your eyes open, you'll notice a lot of people in the Facebook groups we all hang out in, asking for help with their descriptions. Help them. You'll be helping yourself.

Back to my story. I had been assisting authors rewrite descriptions for about six months, and they were reporting great improvements in their conversion rates. Some of them were doing better than my books.

Did I ask myself why?

Did I realize that maybe my own descriptions could be improved?

No. I assumed it was simply a case of their books being written in different genres. My descriptions, for my genres, were already perfect.

The hubris continued.

One day at the beginning of 2018, about 9 months after I had been doing lots of copywriting for others, the voice in my head asked, "Do you really think you got it right on the first try a year and a half ago... before you did all this other copywriting?"

I understand probabilities.

It didn't seem likely.

I rewrote two of my books that had perfect descriptions. The conversion rate improved by about 20%. That's a big number.

You must practice copywriting.

With time will come improvement.

In six months, you'll want to rewrite all your descriptions again.

Note: **Do NOT** rewrite them every time you panic about your sales. Reread the section on variance. Always give the new description time to have enough clicks to truly understand its effectiveness.

CHAPTER SEVEN

WHITE SPACE MATTERS.

In the newspaper business, one wants their article to be "above the fold." That's the most important real estate. It would stand to reason that one wants to pack as much into that tiny few lines as possible on Amazon.

Don't do it.

Focus on a few short hooks.

We want them to click "read more."

Most people will click it regardless, so putting all sorts of important things about your book above the fold isn't necessary. Remember, your description is being judged by more than just the words. There is a certain look that will be most appealing.

You'll notice all the descriptions we analyze in this book have similar layouts. They're not identical, but the general theme is short, short, short, small paragraph, short, short, small paragraph, etc. Pay attention to the way it looks.

Be warned, one can overdo the short, too. If all the rows contain single lines of text without any two to three-line paragraphs breaking up the visual, then it's just as bad as a single block of text.

Remember, formatting is important.

CHAPTER EIGHT

Don't Panic and Analyze.
You're going to make changes.
A new description comes with fear.
Authors love two things:

1. When we make it full-time, each day is pants-optional.
2. Panicking.

Let's talk about expectations. It may help you avoid arriving at the conclusion that the description changes you just made didn't work and that it reflects poorly on you as a person. And also, that you probably aren't fit to be a parent, and liver failure is now a distinct possibility because the only rational course of action is to start drinking like a gaggle of soccer moms on a weeknight when the kids are all away on some sort of school outing.

The typical author, when found in the wild, is a frightened creature who startles easily.

They will make a change to their description and start watching their dashboard. It's a common belief that any new thing they try will be the magic "easy" button that launches their book to the top of the overall ranking on Amazon, get them a movie deal, and ultimately lead to parties at the home of A-list celebrities.

Four out of five dentists, who write books in their spare time, have said they will give a test four minutes to prove it works before going back to what wasn't working and sticking with it for the next twenty years.

Sadly, this thinking may be slightly off the mark.

Here's why…

Note: I'm about to use a word from the lexicon of mathematics. If you read this word, you will NOT be transported into your high-school algebra class with the middle-aged balding teacher whose fondness for garlic makes afternoon classes aromatically intolerable… just don't read the word ALOUD three times. If you do that—well, I can't be held responsible.

The word is variance.

It's not necessary that you know how to do the math to calculate variance; it's just important to understand the concept from a very high level.

Let's take the sales for *Mastering Amazon Ads: An Author's Guide* for the last ten days.

Ebook sales : 1, 3, 1, 5, 3, 9, 2, 4, 8, 4
Print sales: 3, 5, 3, 0, 0, 1, 2, 2, 0, 4

Do you see how much it changes from day to day?

That's variance.

In this case, the variance is 6.6 pm the ebook sales and 2.8 on the print sales. You do NOT need to know how to calculate that, though it is easy in Excel. (I used Var.P, which calculates variance on the entire population.)

Again, and I can't stress this enough, the previous bit of math doesn't need to be calculated, but it does need to be understood to the extent that the number of sales changes from one day to the next.

Does that make sense?

Let's move on and talk about another important concept… not wearing pants.

It's liberating.

No, wait. That's not what I wanted to focus on. It's page reads.

They are a lagging metric.

Now you may not know what I mean by the term lagging metric, so let me explain it using the Socratic method… in Latin.

Okay, I won't use Latin, but I will try to teach you this concept by busting out a page from Socrates's playbook, *How to Make Authors Learn Stuff and Other Feats of Amazing Prestidigitation.*

So, I want you to imagine 1,000 people over the last year have downloaded your book through KU.

And each one of them sent you a piece of fan mail saying two things: 1. they love your writing, and 2. it took them x days to read it.

Did 100% of the people read your book in 1 day?

From looking at all the responses, are there some people who read more slowly than other, maybe taking a week or a month to read it?

If you make a change to a description, and you're running ads, and you want to know if it is converting better or not, do you need to wait for a while to allow the KU readers a chance to finish?

IMPORTANT: Raise your hand if I lost you on this last question or if you answered "yes" because you were guessing and it seemed like that was the answer I was looking for.

We should back up and talk about how to calculate conversion rate, first.

This may get a little bit mathy, but it's crucial to your success, so read it slowly and multiple times, if that's what's needed for it to make sense. Also, I'm going to give you the simplest way to judge the Before and After of your description.

Now because the length of a book factors into how long it takes for a person to read it, and because the longer it takes, the more days you want to allow, this example will be for a book of 300 KENPC.

Step 1: For the 30 days prior to the change of the description and the 30 days following (it might be best, since the description will go live during one day, to not include that day) gather the number of sales and, if you're Amazon-exclusive, the number of page reads.

Step 2: Divide the number of page reads by the KENPC number and round up to the nearest whole number.

For example, let's say that before the change you had 128,432 page reads on the book (in thirty days). Divide that number by 300 (our example KENPC number), and you get 428.1 KU download equivalents. We'll round this up to 429 because there's no such thing as one-tenth of a person.

Step 3: Add up all the paid clicks you had for both time periods.

(**IMPORTANT:** If you are NOT yet doing any paid advertising then you can't do this analysis.)

Step 4: Add Sales and KU Downloads together for both groups.

Step 5: Divide the total paid clicks by the number of conversions (Step 4).

Step 6: Compare Before and After.

EXAMPLE

Before Clicks: 5,000
Before Conversions: 166
Conversion Rate = 30.1, or as I like to say 1:30 (read one-in-thirty) meaning it took 30 clicks to get a sale or download.

After Clicks: 2,000
After Conversions: 86
Conversion Rate = 23.25 or 1:23.25

There is one important thing to realize—and this is where most people go off the rails—you *must* look at conversion rates.

That's the ONLY number that matters.

If a person stops at conversions then they would think that 166 is better than 86, but they would horribly wrong. Does this make sense?

It isn't about how many sales we get. It's about how many we get with the fewest possible number of paid clicks. Paying for 23 to get a new reader is vastly better than paying for 30. That's what we're trying to learn.

So again, in this example, the After was better than the Before.

You have no idea how many times I've done the math for authors who drew the wrong conclusions because they only looked at conversions, or worse… much worse, they only looked at sales. When this happens, it makes me want to go on a tri-state killing spree. So, if you value the lives of people in Massachusetts, Wisconsin, and California, please don't get lazy on your analysis.

IMPORTANT:
REREAD THIS CHAPTER NOW.

I know your eyes glossed over when you saw there were numbers, but this will make you better at running your business.

CHAPTER NINE

Now the good stuff.

Please read all the descriptions. Don't just jump ahead to one what looks like it is in your genre. That's cheating. There's no crying in baseball or cheating in learning copywriting.

Each chapter has the original description by the author, as they were sent to me. Some of them have two. I analyze each of them. Sometimes there is mockery. But what's important is that just because you may not write science fiction, it doesn't mean you won't learn something.

So, read them all.

It's a lot of descriptions, but you're trying to sell books. Trust me, I'm a trained cable TV installer. (Note: I really am)

CHAPTER TEN

DESCRIPTION ONE - SCIENCE FICTION
Let's look at a description.

The theme here might be, "If at first you don't succeed, dig deeper."

Jason reached out to me through Facebook. He had just bought my course and wanted to talk about his description. I told him to send me the original.

He did one better. He sent the original and his first attempt at writing one that was more in line with what I teach in my Mastering Amazon Ads course.

The first bit is what he wrote, and then the third version is the one I created based upon the first two. I'll interject my thoughts in italics.

History:

"I've been battling with this product description for two years now. I've re-written it many times, and never gotten a decent, profitable conversion rate."

IMPORTANT TO NOTE, HE HAD *NOT*
HAD A PROFITABLE CONVERSION RATE.

"As of yesterday, I had a blurb which I then rewrote after watching your video on rewriting your product description. I'll give you the before and after.

(I added that I'm a philosopher in the second version – I have a PhD in Philosophy. Maybe I shouldn't have mentioned it. I'm not sure.)"

Author: Jason Werbeloff
Title: *Defragmenting Daniel: The Organ Scrubber*
Price: $4.99
Genre: Science Fiction

Before:

They harvested his organs. Now he'll reap what they've sown.

The Gutter orphanage, 2064. As a child, Daniel had no choice but to trade his body parts for room and board. Now more synthetic than human, he's barely survived to see his 18th birthday. Finally, free from captivity, he uncovers the terrible truth of his origins… and an unfulfilled legacy of revenge.

Daniel's organs still live on in the bodies of the powerful elite who stole his childhood. And he won't stop until he's harvested every last one. To reclaim his rightful parts, he's forced to cross over into a heavily fortified and unfamiliar world. With the authorities hot on his trail, Daniel must fulfill his bloody quest before his broken body takes its final breath.

Defragmenting Daniel: The Organ Scrubber is the first book in a provocative sci-fi thriller trilogy. If you like high-tech dystopian worlds, eccentric characters, and pulse-pounding action, then you'll love Jason Werbeloff's visceral novel.

Buy Defragmenting Daniel to dissect a gut-wrenching vision of the not-so-distant future.

Analysis: Jason gets points for having a first line of a hook. But it's too long. By having both sentences on the same line, we're losing what I like to call, "The accidental reading."

This is basically to say that in the incredibly brief time the potential reader lands on the page and is searching for the "read more" link to click, we want to try to get the first hook to register.

I believe it needs to be less than six words so that a person who just happens to glance at it would register the entire hook as if reading a single word.

Pay attention to this theme throughout the book.

After:

They harvested his organs.

Now he'll reap what they've sown.

The Gutter orphanage, 2064. As a child, Daniel had no choice but to trade his body parts for room and board.

Now more synthetic than human, Daniel has barely survived to see his 18th birthday. Finally, free from captivity, he uncovers the terrible truth of his origins... and an unfulfilled legacy of revenge.

Daniel's organs live on in the bodies of the powerful elite who stole his childhood. And he won't stop until he's harvested every last one.

With the authorities hot on his trail, Daniel must fulfill his bloody quest before his broken body takes its final breath.

You'll love this provocative sci-fi thriller by philosopher, Jason Werbeloff, because he knows how to build a mind-bending dystopian world and tell a page-turning story.

Buy Defragmenting Daniel now.

———

Meeks Version (Take One):

They harvested his organs.

Now he'll reap what they've sown.

The Gutter orphanage, 2064. He was poor. Life didn't do him any favors. As a child, Daniel had no choice but to trade his body parts to survive. They were the only things he had of value.

Now more synthetic than human, Daniel has barely survived to see his 18th birthday. Finally, free from captivity, he uncovers the terrible truth of his origins… and an unfulfilled legacy of revenge. The truth is hard to take.

Who received his organs?

Can he find the monsters who preyed on his childhood?

With the authorities hot on his trail, will Daniel be able to finish his quest before time runs out?

You'll love this provocative sci-fi thriller, because everyone enjoys a mind-bending dystopian world that's an amazing page-turner.

Buy *Defragmenting Daniel* now.

———

Result: Failure

I wanted to start with this example because many of you will have the same result with your first try. Jason came to me about a month after we had made the change. The conversion rate may have improved slightly, but it was not the great improvement we wanted.

What had been the problem?

Personally, I had found the whole "harvested organs" bit a little bit grue-some, but I'm not his readership. I took for granted that we should be focusing on this aspect of the book. Now, with the results being in and clearly people weren't more interested in buying the book, I asked him if we could tone it down.

Give the next version a read. We focused on his being an orphan more than on his parts. It's a better description, now. The bold, spacing and CTA were not my original suggestion, but I encourage all authors to test their own ideas.

———

New Version (Take Two):

In a world where orphans are discarded…

One young man must take up the fight.

The Gutter orphanage, 2064. As a child, Daniel had no choice but to trade his body parts for room and board. Now more synthetic than human, he's barely survived to see his 18th birthday.

Daniel's body is failing.

The gears in his knee grind, his synthetic cornea weeps, and his 3D-printed lungs spasm in winter.

Daniel can't afford new synthetics. He needs the organs he was born with. But their new owners won't return them.
Not without a fight.

Defragmenting Daniel: The Organ Scrubber is the first book in a provocative sci-fi thriller trilogy. If you like high-tech dystopian worlds with pulse-pounding action, then you'll love Jason Werbeloff's visceral novel.

Buy *Defragmenting Daniel* to dissect a gut-wrenching vision of the not-so-distant future.

CHAPTER ELEVEN

DESCRIPTION TWO - DYSTOPIAN

Author: MK Harkings
Title: *The Reader (Immortal Series Book 1)*
Price: .99
Genre: Dystopian

Before:

Hunted, shot, and without her memory, eighteen-year-old Ann Baker wakes in shallow water on a deserted Pacific Northwest island. She is soon approached by two young men claiming to be her friends. Something isn't right, but when gunshots sound, Ann is left with little choice but to allow Devon and Archer to help her escape. Soon she finds herself in their North Bend mountain compound, where the higher evolved humans claim to be mind-readers. While Ann heals, she realizes they believe her to be one of the last and most powerful of all – The Lost One. She's welcomed by most with opened arms, but not everyone is happy about her arrival. A jealous adversary has plans for Ann, which spirals the entire Reader community into chaos.

She's welcomed by most with opened arms, but not everyone is happy about her arrival. A jealous adversary has plans for Ann, which spirals the entire Reader community into chaos.

As lies, murder, and betrayal threaten to rip apart the once harmonious mountain dwellers, Ann is thrust into making a decision that could save or devastate not only The Readers, but all of mankind. But there's just one glitch: by doing so it may require her to make the ultimate sacrifice.

Analysis:

Do you want to read the giant block of text?

Nor do I. That being said, there are some good bits in the first line —"hunted, shot, memory loss, and deserted island"—that might be good hook fodder.

There are also some extra words that aren't needed. Do we need her last name? If it's a deserted island, and then the next sentence has two people approach her, there's a bit of a disconnect. And I don't like "soon" as it isn't needed.

In copywriting, we want to be short and concise. I will say this a bunch: copywriting is not prose.

As we continue to read through these giant blocks of text, we get the sense that the entire story is laid before us. Yes, this is a detailed synopsis of what appears to be most of the book. MK Harkings has left us little to discover.

And there isn't a call-to-action.

This description needs help.

Data:

I don't have data on all of the descriptions we will discuss, but when I do, I'll share it.

The original description, from Nov 4 - Nov 10, had 1,367 clicks. As such, we can analyze the effectiveness of the original description with regard to the conversion rate.

Clicks = 1367
Sales = 40
KU Download Estimate = 9 (2970/338 = 8.78, which we round up to 9)

1453/47 = 1:29.65

This is NOT good for a 99-cent book.

Meeks Version (Take One):

What was that pain?

Amy, shot and dazed, saw them running toward her.

Did she know these two men?

They acted like friends. She heard more shots and decided now wasn't the time to figure things out. Down the beach, they ran. The fog of her memory made it all seem unreal. What was she getting into? Who was chasing them?

Amy's life might never be the same. For weeks she healed, but still the memories are gone. All she knows about the world is this tiny mountain community she finds herself in, and it's clear there's something going on. There are rumors about who she might be. Is she truly The One, or is it all a con? She has no idea.

Her story is just beginning.

Is Amy a guest or a prisoner?

You'll love this Dystopian adventure, because everyone wants to survive.

Get it now.

Analysis: I think I can do better. This is just a gut feeling. I wrote it when I was tired and now, rereading it, an idea has begun to form. So, I'm going to try again. This is how the description-writing process goes. Second or third attempts may be a big leap forward.

Meeks Version (Take Two):

It still hurt...

...and she still couldn't remember.

Two weeks since someone shot Amy, she lay in a strange mountain village thinking. The men who had found her on the beach said she was their friend, but she was starting to wonder. There were a lot of whispers.

A woman knows when another is jealous. The looks, the curt comments, and the false veneer around others made it clear that Amy was in her crosshairs, but Amy still couldn't remember anything. Who was this woman and what was it all about?

Then it happened…

…one person came to her.

They called her a "Reader" and wanted Amy to make a decision.

In a devastated world, a new era has begun, and the future depends on one young woman. Will it be more than she can bear?

You'll love this Dystopian adventure, because everyone loves a battle against all odds.

Get it now.

Analysis:

I like this one better. It doesn't tell much beyond what's important. It's dystopian, the protagonist is Amy, and someone is out to get her. It hints at something called a "Reader," which is a good hook.

CHAPTER TWELVE

Author: Lora Edward
Title: *1888 The Ripper File*
Price: $0.99
Genre: Paranormal Mystery

Before:

With a love of all things dark and mysterious, history professor Teagan Faelynn is obsessed with the lore of Jack the Ripper.

Not one just to enjoy the legend for what it is, Teagan travels to London at the behest of her grandfather in order to study a new journal with possible answers to history's most intriguing questions. What Teagan finds instead is more than just a new lead--but a world set apart from ours in every way imaginable. For not only is Jack the Ripper real--but every conceivable monster known to man or myth: dragons, fairies, witches, Valkyries abound in a world where the truth is often too incredible to be believed. Now hundreds of years in the past and beset on all sides by friends and foes, Teagan must guard her life--and her heart--from all the dangers 1888 London has to offer and dive headfirst into the secrets of the past. For learning the Ripper's identity is merely the beginning--when the killer himself comes calling--and drags Teagan into the most incredible adventure of her young life.

Step into the past with Teagan in the first installment of the series and rip into a paranormal romance so thrilling it's to die for...

Analysis:

Another giant block of text.

Meeks Version:

Was the journal the key?

Would her obsession get her killed?

The streets of London have never been more dangerous.

Teagan's grandfather had found it. What sort of clues would the journal hold? As a renowned expert on Jack the Ripper, she was eager to take a look. Be careful what you wish for—it may not work out the way you hoped.

The streets have shadows. Muffled footsteps seemed to follow. On a cold, wet night, Teagan's imagination seemed to get the best her. When you study monsters, it can be easy to get a fright, but is the threat real?

Will she find the answers she needs?

Is it worth it?

You'll adore this paranormal mystery, because everyone enjoys an adventure.

Get it now.

Analysis:

I took elements of the original and ripped out the details to make it more of a mystery. The formatting is much stronger. The description is now much less "heavy" than it was with the giant block of text.
Readers will be more likely to give it a chance.

CHAPTER THIRTEEN

THE CAKE AT THE END OF THE TUNNEL.

We all work really hard. Writing books and getting them to market takes a lot of effort. It can take years to get to that "It's time to quit my day job moment."

When it happens, it's wonderful.

My moment happened three years ago. I love this life.

Last weekend, though, something even better happened.

I was born in Columbus, Ohio. My father was finishing his Ph.D., and mom was a nurse. A couple of years later, without consulting me at all, a sister was added to the mix.

It turned out to be okay.

There are few things I'm more thankful for than having loving parents... who like math. They made growing up wonderful.

In little league, my dad was the manager for many years. He would throw batting practice to me until his arm nearly fell off. Dad taught me golf.

And he taught me MATH!

It's the latter that's been the most important.

Well, this year he turns 80 on November 21.

Dad and I have watched a lot of college football together over the years. We cheer for ISU because that's where he was a professor and where I graduated.

The Cyclones are our second favorite team.

The Ohio State Buckeyes hold the top spot. When I lived in Iowa, just a few hours away, I'd often drive to Mom and Dad's on football Saturdays to watch the Buckeyes.

Now, though, I live in Las Vegas... and football season is about to begin.

I'm excited... and a little sad... maybe even lonely, thinking about not being able to watch the games with Dad. (Note: Mom watches, too, but she mostly likes to wait until the fourth quarter because it's just too tense to watch the whole game.)

Well, this weekend I did something cool that was made possible by the book business.

It's the best reason EVER (for me) to have worked so hard.

As I said, Dad turns 80 on November 21st. I'm planning on going home to be there. And I bought him a present, one which I couldn't have afforded in other years before I was an author.

But this year, because I ran a sale on this thing I sell, I could afford to pick up a pair of tickets to the Ohio State vs. michigan game, the biggest game of the season for Buckeye fans. And it's three days after his birthday!!!

(Editing Nazis, michigan is NEVER capitalized when you're from Columbus.)

I bought the tickets on Stub Hub. They were expensive, and that's okay... because the sale is going well.

The hotel is booked.

He will NEVER see this present coming.

I'm just giddy at the thought of the expression on his face.

Not that birthday present-giving is a competition... but... I've won.

The point is, we work hard. It can be easy to get lost in all the STUFF.

But at the end of the day, it isn't about the money; it's about the memories that having a little extra cash can make happen.

So, thanks, everyone.

It's because of the support you wonderful authors that I'm going to give my dad the best birthday present EVER.

And when we're eating the birthday cake and opening the presents, I'll know that it was all made possible because I worked hard and kept at it.

It may be a long tunnel, but you'll get there, too.

CHAPTER FOURTEEN

DESCRIPTION FOUR - YA FANTASY

Author: Bethany Hoeflich
Title: *Dreg (The Dreg Trilogy book one)*
Price: $3.99
Genre: YA Fantasy

Before:

Mara is dirt— worse, actually. She's a dreg.

Nineteen-year-old Mara has spent her whole life wondering why the old Magi refused to awaken her Gift. With no magical ability to call her own, Mara faces a life of persecution with no value, no power and no purpose.

When a charming new Magi arrives in her village of Stonehollow, Mara expects more of the same. Instead, she's thrust into a dangerous tangle of secrets and lies that will shatter everything she thought she knew.

Now, Mara must flee the Order— a powerful organization of Magi who will do anything to capture her before she can expose the truth.

Analysis:

This is a better-than-average description from the start. The opening is a solid hook, but could it be better? The paragraphs are the right length. She needs a CTA, though, and we want to bring the reader in with "You" and "Because."

Meeks Version:

The Order has found out.

Mara has a choice…

Flee or fight.

And nobody beats The Order. At nineteen years old, she's lost without her gift. The magi must awaken it, but they don't like Dregs. She's a dreg, and they treat her like dirt. But she knows a secret, and with that comes power.

Will it be enough to save her?

She'd better find a friend.

There's a new Magi in her village. He's charming. But can she trust him? Will he help her?

Time is running out… will she figure out her next move before The Order hunts her down?

You'll love this YA Fantasy, because of the twists and turns.

Get it now.

Analysis:

In my humble opinion, this version has more hooks. Starting with The Order, and since I don't say what they've "found out," that's a bit of a hook. Again, the original version is pretty solid, but I do believe this will convert better. Only time and analysis will tell.

CHAPTER FIFTEEN

DESCRIPTION FIVE - YA

Author: N.M. Howell
Title: *Marked by Dragon's Blood: A Young Adult High Fantasy Adventure (Return of the Dragonborn Book 1)*
Price: $4.99
Genre: Young Adult

Before:

Descended from Dragons. Condemned to Death. Destined for Glory. Death and secrecy. No strangers to Andie Rogers.

Ripped from the dying arms of her dragonborn mother, Andie had to use the sorcery inherited from her father to disguise her own dragon's blood magic. Now a teenager, she must master her wizardry. The University is the center of magic and the government in Arvall City; a place that will teach her how to become a fully-fledged sorcerer.

For one of the last remaining dragonborn, it's also a place of immeasurable danger.

Haunted by dreams of her tormented ancestors, Andie is compelled to answer their call and discover the truth of her race's destruction, but it can only be found in the world's magical capital, populated by powerful sorcerers determined to uphold the lie at all cost. Should they discover dragonborn blood pulses through her veins, death will be swift, and her people will never be redeemed.

Will Andie survive the impossible task and shatter the lies under which the world lives? Will she finally release her people from the shackles that bind them?

From a USA Today bestseller comes a thrilling high fantasy adventure filled with dragons and laced with deception. A coming of age tale for the ages. Escape into this exciting young adult fantasy series readers are hailing as a "fun mix of Harry Potter and Eragon." Scroll up and click into this magical world today.

"Definitely a mix of Eragon and Harry Potter. Great cast of characters excellent story plenty of magic action good and evil. Mix in a little bit of prejudice and bias and see what causes the hatred and how these characters work their way through it and reach their goal. Magical mystical world at its best. Definitely you must check it out." – 5-star Amazon Review

"Wow. It doesn't matter what walk of life we are from we all need to fight for what we believe in." – 5-star Amazon Review

"Howell is a master storyteller who weaves fast paced tales while creating a fantastic world with amazing characters." – 5-star Amazon Review

"This is one of those books that keeps you up at night because you tell yourself **one more chapter again and again!**" – 5-star Amazon Review

Analysis:

There's a lot of information here. I give her high marks for the bolding. A lot of the description, though, is a detailed synopsis of what is going to happen in the book. Also, the sheer volume of description will cause some potential readers to move on without giving it a chance. People just can't be bothered to read a massive description.

Meeks Version:

Everyone has secrets…

…but Andie's brings with it danger.

How will she learn the Dragon Blood Magic she needs?

At the University in Arvall city, teachers show young people how to use magic, but not everyone can attend. And Dragon Born magic is all but dead. Is she the last one? Why was her race all but destroyed?

Andie is caught between wanting to learn magic and fearing for her life if anyone finds out who she really is. As she searches for answers, each night her dreams haunt her. The future of her race seems to be resting on her shoulders…but where to begin.

Will she find answers and be able to expose the truth?

You'll love this high fantasy adventure, because everyone loves dragons, deception, and intrigue.

Get it now.

From a USA Today bestseller comes a thrilling high fantasy adventure filled with dragons and laced with deception. A coming of age tale for the ages. Escape into this exciting young adult fantasy series readers are hailing as a "fun mix of Harry Potter and Eragon." Scroll up and click into this magical world today.

"Definitely a mix of Eragon and Harry Potter. Great cast of characters excellent story plenty of magic action good and evil. Mix in a little bit of prejudice and bias and see what causes the hatred and how these characters work their way through it and reach their goal. Magical mystical world at its best. Definitely you must check it out." – 5-star Amazon Review

"Wow. It doesn't matter what walk of life we are from we all need to fight for what we believe in." – 5-star Amazon Review

"Howell is a master storyteller who weaves fast paced tales while creating a fantastic world with amazing characters." – 5-star Amazon Review

"This is one of those books that keeps you up at night because you tell yourself one more chapter again and again!" – 5-star Amazon Review

Analysis:

I trimmed it down a bit. Also, I set the final section with the quotes apart with a couple of blank lines.

For those who want to read the endorsements, they're there, but for those who just want to read the description, the extra stuff is in its own section and doesn't make the description feel so daunting. A description should be easy to consume.

CHAPTER SIXTEEN

DESCRIPTION SIX - CHRISTIAN WESTERN

Author: Susan Leigh Carlton
Title: *A Life Restarted: Romance After Forty (I Won't Marry You Book 2)*
Price: $3.49
Genre: Christian Western

Before:

Can a woman find love and romance after forty?

Abigail Ashley's life turned upside down when her husband carried out his despicable plan. After he died in prison, she is convinced she was unworthy of any decent person. She lived only for her daughter and grandson.

Brady Lucas was so overwhelmed with grief and guilt after the tragic death of his beloved wife, he left Texas, leaving his young daughter with his parents in Comanche Springs and had no plans for their future.

When he met Abigail his whole world changed.

Can their two matchmaking daughters overcome his stubborn pride and her feelings of low self esteem and bring them together? Can the tiny spark between them be fanned into a flame or will they be left in a life with no love and romance?

Analysis:

The first concern is the series title (I Won't Marry You Book 2). This sounds like it's screaming NO HEA, which I believe is the kiss of death for most genres of romance.

Meeks Version:

She turned forty…

…and was alone.

This wasn't how it was supposed to be.

Abigal's life took a wrong turn. It wasn't her fault. He'd died. Now she was alone and full of doubt. But one must go on when they have children. Would she ever find a way to love herself again?

The crushing weight of grief was too much. How would Brady carry the guilt that came with it? He'd loved her with all his heart, and now he was empty, just struggling to make it through each day.

Two souls desperate for hope…

are so close to meeting…

But will fate get in the way?

For their lives to change, the universe may need a helping hand.

You'll love this unusual romance, because everyone dreams of love.

Get it now.

Analysis:

I removed the references to low self-esteem. They didn't really make the protagonist appealing. It's fine that we learn this about the character when reading the book, but we don't want to drive people away before they buy. I focused more on the question of whether or not they will meet.

CHAPTER SEVENTEEN

ARTICLE - MY HAT

I helped an author…

…and the Universe gave me my hat back.

About an hour ago, I woke up from a lovely nap. My FB DMs were many, and I fired off answers to the questions that had popped up while I slept.

The last person, one of my students, was on the cusp of freaking out.

Authors often freak out.

They're quick to judge their situation hopeless. Usually, it's seven to ten minutes after making a change and not seeing improvement.

Anyone here ever panic?

Well, this is a story of an end to the panic and the near-miraculous appearance of a hat I dearly loved but thought was lost.

A few weeks back, for my father's 80th birthday, I bought him two tickets to the Ohio State vs. michigan game in Columbus. It was an all-expenses-paid bit of quality time with his son.

Best present ever.

The Buckeyes won 62 - 39.

I bought a knit Ohio State hat at the game as a souvenir. Four days ago, I was sure I had dropped it on one of my evening walks.

This crushed me.

The Universe felt my pain.

Anyway, as I wiped the post-nap groggy out of my eyes, took a drink of Fiji water, and hovered my fingers over the keyboard, my mind switched into Author Coaching Man.

A few questions later and I realized where he was mistaken. We needed to talk live. I get wordy, and sometimes chatting in DM is too slow for my level of enthusiasm.

This author was nearing the point of just packing it all in.

Have any of you been there?

Well, you get points for still being HERE (20BooksTo50K). That means you're in the game… you're winning. Well done… I digress.

This author was having doubts. The numbers looked bad (to him), and he hadn't looked at the cover of The Hitchhikers Guide to the Galaxy recently and had forgotten the comforting words printed across it.

To the untrained eye, his numbers did look bad. My eyes are NOT untrained.

It appeared his read-through was awful.

It appeared his conversion rate was awful.

Neither of these things were true; they were a function of time. Too little time, in analysis, is the leading cause of mistaken conclusions and gum disease.

4 out of 5 Dentists recommend Dentyne and letting your data mature long enough to be statistically significant.

We talked at length about the time issue, and he got it. We analyzed his data as best we could, and the indicators were that everything was fine.

Then we looked at his covers. They needed some small tweaks, but they were things he could do himself.

His description was awesome (In the interest of full disclosure, I wrote it, so I may be biased, but the hooks are really good.)

His reviews, 4.5 average, on twenty reviews, for his first book as an author is excellent. He didn't know that.

Still, this author wondered why he shouldn't pack it all in. He couldn't see the bright future that lay in front of him.

I could. I'm a trained data analyst.

We talked about his plans moving forward.

Okay, they needed some tweaking too. He was focused on sales.

This was a mistake.

We talked about his writing schedule. It wasn't optimized either.

By the end of the call, we had laid out his plan for the next six months. We covered writing, editing, launching, and mindset. I even agreed to talk to his wife in January if she needed a pep talk.

He left the call panic-free and full of the optimism that his books deserved.

And the Universe saw that it was good.

My post-preventing-panic enthusiasm made it impossible for me to work. I get really fired up after calls like this. I had to do something drastic.

I started to clean.

The renters insurance bill that I had paid by phone earlier in the day needed to be filed.

I picked it up, and there was my Buckeyes hat.

Had it been there the whole time?

I don't think so. I'm 83% sure the Universe had found it on the Strip four days ago and was waiting until I deserved to get my hat back and then BAM put it under the paperwork.

The moral of the story...

...helping others feels good...

...there's a lot to learn to understand this business, so if you're about to panic, reach out and find someone who can help you understand the Big Picture (this 20booksto50k group is great for that stuff)...

...And lastly, the Universe is a HUGE Ohio State Buckeyes fan and would never let a cherished hat stay lost. (Note: if it had been a michigan hat, it would be still in the gutter... where it belongs.)

Stay positive my friends.

This is a business of numbers, education, and effort. You can all achieve your dreams if you stay in the game.

Go Buckeyes!

CHAPTER EIGHTEEN

Author: MK Meredith
Title: *Love on the Cape: An On the Cape Novel (Cape Van Buren Book 1)*
Price: $0.99
Genre: Contemporary Fiction, Women's Fiction, Sagas

Before:

"Love on the Cape is the kind of romance I love best--sexy, deeply emotional, rooted in characters who have had real lives and real traumas, and find love and healing in each other's arms, all beautifully crafted by a writer with brilliant instincts. Don't miss this one." ~ Barbara O'Neal, seven time RITA award winning author of How to Bake a Perfect Life.

On the rocky, atmospheric coast of Cape Van Buren, Maine…

For far too long, Larkin Sinclair has been seeking solace in her memories rather than living in the present. But when Van Buren Enterprises announces plans to develop historic Cape Van Buren into a gold-plated playground for the wealthy, Larkin refuses to watch one more beautiful thing in her life be destroyed, so she sets out to preserve the historic cape—and with it, the memory of her son. Only it isn't the company she needs to fear, it's the dangerously irresistible CEO who has the power to derail her plans.

Annoyingly arrogant one minute and beautifully wounded the next, he awakens something in her heart that had died with her son even as his actions promise to break it once again.

Ryker Van Buren needs closure from his dark childhood and the best way to do that is to level his family home. As the rightful owner of the estate, he plans on developing it into a master community—what better way to secure his future than by selling off his past? Until he locks eyes with the passionate conservationist who fights him at every turn for the rights to his legacy. He can't keep his hands off her, but worse, he can't get her off his land or out of his dreams.

Attraction sparks and two broken souls recognize each other through the pain. Against all odds, love blooms on the cape. But when their pasts collide, will they choose love in the moment, or will they lose their chance at forever?

Analysis:

This book has 68 reviews with an average of 4.8 stars. That means it's a really good book. We're giving it an A+. I'm not that familiar with her genre, but I really like the cover. I give it an A, too.

The description... well, the kindest thing I can say about it is that if we compare it to the 25 million people Chairman Mao let die in building his communist regime, the description is only slightly less of a war crime... by about one percent.

Once we get past the really long quote, which is actually quite nice, but is definitely NOT only six words, we get to the opening line. The spot where we would expect the first hook. And what do we find?

"It was a dark and stormy night," or words to that effect. This cliché is so bad in literature as to have spawned a contest where this cliché is mocked with reckless abandon.

This is not how we start a description.

After reporting the opening line to the people in charge of such things at the Hague, I read the rest of the description. It's just a synopsis of what happens in the book in painful detail.

We can do better.

Meeks Version:

Living in the past is easy…

But that's a slippery slope.

Can she find a way to restart her life and find happiness?

It was a simple thing. It caught Larkin's attention, and she needed to act. Plans were being developed for her town, and she feared the worst. Who is this Ryker guy, and why is he trying to ruin her city?

He had a vision. The estate from Ryker's childhood would be the perfect spot to develop his grand plan for the community. The details were all worked out. He'd thought of everything… but he didn't count on some woman getting in his way. And why did she have to be so damn good looking?

Is there something deeper going on?

A moment of spark and their lives may never be the same.

But it isn't going to be easy. The past has a way of ruining everything.

Can they beat the odds?

You'll love this contemporary fiction because of its depth and surprises.

Get it now.

Analysis:

I stripped out a lot of the unnecessary details. We don't need their full names. It's not important to give Ryker's backstory. The original description simply told us too much. I kept it simple. The hooks keep one engaged in the description until the end. It is much less war crime-y.

CHAPTER NINETEEN

Author: Nicole Marie
Title: *A Bitten Curse (Darkness Bites Book 1)*
Price: $0.99
Genre: Erotic Paranormal Suspense with Reverse Harem Twist

Before:

I came to London to kill vampires. I failed.

I woke up in my apartment days after our failed mission, alone and near death. Well, alone apart from the vampire King who has been in my head since he bit me that night.

I don't know how our minds became linked or how I survived that night when the rest of my team did not, but I've been in hiding for my life ever since.

My life now revolves around two things: staying alive and pissing off the bloodsucker in my head.

The only thing that drives him crazier than drinking myself unconscious? F**king shifters.

Analysis:

Not all descriptions are war crimes. I like this one, but I think it could be a little better. I have to admit, though, I have a personal bias against descriptions in first person. My preference is third.

This is not to say there's anything wrong with first person. There might be, but I don't have any statistically significant proof and have never done an A/B test to find out. It would likely be such a small difference, if one were better than the other, that I'd be hard-pressed to make my case.

So, that's a study for another day… or never.

Let's take a look at what I believe is an improvement. You be the judge.

Meeks Version:

There was a problem…

…Vampires in London.

She came to kill them… and failed.

Could things get any worse? The bite marks she woke up with made her think they could. It was going to be a bad day. She noticed a touch of death coming on. How had she even survived?

And where was the Vampire King now?

Then it happened. The pain, shooting from the back of her head. Blood filled her eyes, and for a moment, everything spun. An instant later, the eyes she looked through were not her own. And what she saw chilled her to the bone.

It wasn't about winning now…

…it was about survival

But how?

You'll love this genre-busting adventure, because it's a finely woven tale with all the best bits you adore.

Get it now.

Analysis:

My version goes a little further with the humor. I loved the "I failed," bit so I took it further with the comment about "a touch of death coming on." Most of what I wrote came from her description, but I did it a little bit differently.

Instead of saying she "mind-linked" with the Vampire King, I hinted that there was a "mind link," but didn't say with whom. That makes it more of a hook. Then I added my "You'll… because" and used "genre-busting" to address all of the crossover and set expectations that this would be a little different than what people are used to reading.

Lastly, I dropped in the CTA.

CHAPTER TWENTY

DESCRIPTION NINE - HARD SCIENCE FICTION

Author: Bill Patterson
Title: *Riddled Space*
Price: .99
Genre: Hard Science Fiction, Colonization, Space Exploration

Before:

The gruesome death of the Moonbase Collins's chief sets the professional UN Astronaut Corps against the United Nations Space Operations Command and its oily Director General when he attempts to sell . It's not quite a mutiny, but the corrupt head of UNSOC is determined to crush any sense of independent action by the willful astronauts, especially the new commander of the UN Space Station Roger B. Chaffee, Lisa Daniels. All of the workers 'upstairs', in orbit and on the Moon, are under the gun--the work is hard, dangerous, and unrelenting. The morale budget is cut to the bone, the only luxuries are the ones that the shuttle pilots can smuggle up, the vendors using the manufacturing space are being squeezed for bribes at every turn.

Then a massive explosion rocks the South Polar region of the Moon, spewing radiation and a huge volume of rock into cis-lunar space. Fifteen minutes after the blast, Moonbase Collins falls silent.

Lisa Daniels and her crew are in incredible danger. Not only have they absorbed radiation equivalent to ten-thousand X-rays, they may be in path of the debris plume blasted off of the Moon. The Director-General, faced with losing the source of his bribe money, has forbidden evacuation of the Chaffee. Besides, he has spent his twenty years of rule squeezing the maximum amount of cash from the Chaffee. Non-essentials, like lifeboats, were never funded.

Lisa has a plan to get everyone to Earth, but to put it in action, she will have to sacrifice everything she has worked so hard for all of her life, as well as drag in everyone else on the ground into her mutiny. The real question is: dare she do it?

Analysis:

Read the first line of the description out loud.

I'm serious, I want you (the author reading this) to actually use your vocal cords. There's an important lesson here and I want it to sink in.

It's a mouthful. And "Collins's" is hard to say. Additionally, there is a space before the end stop. And, that first sentence, aside from being so long it made me want to kill myself, is not a hook. It's not even interesting. It's just bad.

And then the horror continues. The rest of the description, which, if I counted correctly, is just seven pages short of being the same length as the Iliad and appears to give away the entire book's plot.

The points here are twofold:

1. I like being snarky… but you knew that.
2. If you struggle to read a line or a word or a strange name, the potential reader may have to stop and try to figure it out too.

We do not want them stopping. We want them to be hooked and glide through the description with ease so they can click that button and start on their journey to becoming a fan.

(**Note:** A good copywriter would have written… "we want them to be hooked and buy the book," but I like getting wordy from time to time. And this is NOT a description, it's my analysis.)

Meeks Version:

How could they have known?

The explosion was massive.

Fifteen minutes later, Moonbase Collins went silent.

In a world of politics and double-dealing, Lisa is just trying to do her job. The lives of her crew are in her hands. The fight for independence was almost too much, but now there's a debris field approaching... and seconds matter.

Choices must be made.

Colonization is never easy.

In a room, far from the explosion, the Director General looks at a monitor. This was not the plan. Who could he make the scapegoat? And then there's the matter of the dissidents. But he has a few cards left to play.

You'll love this hard science fiction novel, because space exploration has never been more exciting.

Get it now.

Analysis:

You'll notice I tell little about the story. My focus was on two aspects of the story. The opposing sides of Lisa and the Director General, though I don't explicitly spell that out.

We don't want to spell things out. We want the potential reader's mind to start to work it out for themselves and get just close enough that they're not sure... so they need to buy (or download) the book to find out.

CHAPTER TWENTY-ONE

ARTICLE - EPIC FAIL

It was an epic fail...

...or was it?

Several years ago, back when I still had a day job, I got a Bookbub promotion. At the time, for my mystery series (one of the larger categories) I'd had about 9 previous promotions.

My best result was making it to #3 overall.

This time would be different. I had a plan. Number one seemed possible.

The night before, I was too excited to sleep. I did what I always do: I worked on my book business to-do list.

I finally went to bed.

The next day, I got up shortly before the email blast went out. I was excited.

Bookbub days are always exciting.

Out of the gate, my downloads per minute (I track the downloads every 15 minutes for the entire day) were the best I'd ever had.

At 4:00 it happened. My 4th book in the Henry Wood Detective series hit #1 overall.

I was thrilled... for 10 minutes.

My book, which had a 4.6 average on about 60 reviews, got a 1-star review.

The person simply said they got the wrong book.

What?

A few minutes later, another 1-star review landed.

My heart sank. I went to the Look Inside feature. The world stopped.

At 3:30 am, when I was working on my to-do list, I fixed a mistake in the first book in my satire series. I uploaded it on KDP... to the 4th book in the Henry Wood series.

40,000 copies of the WRONG book had already been downloaded.

There were tears.

The correct book was uploaded, but we all know it doesn't happen immediately. The downloads continued.

I wrote Amazon and explained what happened.

More 1-star reviews came in.

Within an hour, my BEST book, with its 4.6 average, plummeted to 3.7.

More tears.

I had destroyed my best book.

Amazon, to their credit, got the correct book live inside of an hour. They also agreed to blast out the book to those who had downloaded it.

But the damage was done.

After a few hours of debilitating sadness, I got to work.

I replied to every one-star review and explained what I had done.

I said I was sorry.

It was all I could do.

It was the worst day, which turned into the worst week, as I watched my review average slip to 3.5.

It was an epic fail.

But you know what?

I survived. Over time some of the 1-star reviews were changed. More 5-star reviews came in and it bounced back to 4.1.

The world didn't end.

I kept writing books. I eventually did well enough to quit my day job. Now I'm living my own personal dream author life (some writing, some teaching, and lots of research and analysis).

The worst thing I can imagine, ultimately, had little impact on my ability to reach my goal of "Full-Time Author."

We all have bad days.

Sometimes a review disappears.

Other days someone says they hate our books.

Don't let it stop you.

We Indies can handle anything.

As long as you don't quit, you've got a great chance of success.

CHAPTER TWENTY-TWO

DESCRIPTION TEN - POST-APOCALYPTIC

Author: Chris Muhlenfeld
Title: *Crash: Book 1 of The Obsolescence Trilogy*
Price: $4.99
Genre: Action & Adventure, Science Fiction/Post-Apocalyptic

Before:

The global power and communications outage arrives without warning, taking both civilian and military infrastructures with it. No alien ships darken the skies; no invading armies appear on the horizons. Still, the technological glue that was holding civilization together suddenly vanished, and the world found itself in an uncontrolled freefall. Unexplainable phenomena soon begin appearing all over the planet, deepening the mystery.

James and Alexa watch all this unfolding from their AI-powered rural ranch far from the chaos and destruction. They band together with their quirky neighbors, forming a tight community that shares resources and collective security while the world around them crumbles into unmitigated apocalypse. Together, they begin to investigate the phenomena that mysteriously started appearing overnight. Everywhere. Like magic.

Could the unfolding apocalypse be a blessing in disguise, the beginning of the next leap in human evolution? Or is it the beginning of humanity's final stumble into the shadows of extinction?

Set in the near future where technology has solved most of the world's problems, Crash is the first book in The Obsolescence Trilogy. Plausible, fast-paced and full of rich, insightful characters, this sci-fi thriller will keep you up well past your bedtime. Get it now!

Analysis:

After a good deal of thought into how to describe my complex feelings after reading the description, I wrote down on a yellow legal pad all the things I wanted to discuss. I don't want to be too long winded in my break down. I'm going to try to keep it under 5,000 words.

Meh.

Okay. That gets to the heart of the matter. Let's see if we can do better.

Meeks Version:

And then it went dark…

…the world's electrical grid was gone.

Who would survive the chaos?

James and Alexa saw it unfold from their ranch, which was a blessing. They were away from the chaos, and they thought they were safe. They thought wrong.

What will they do?

All across the country, cities are in crisis.

Logan and his family look out of their Manhattan penthouse. The world is crumbling before Logan's eyes. Unprepared, he's got to do something. They can't stay. But how can they leave, and where will they go?

Someone has a solution.

It's Logan's domestic android.

Can he believe a machine?

You won't believe the twists and turns, but you'll love the adventure.

Get it now.

Analysis:

Can *you* see the difference?

CHAPTER TWENTY-THREE

DESCRIPTION ELEVEN - SCIENCE FICTION

Author: Chris Tickner
Title: *The Humanarium*
Price: $2.99
Genre: Science Fiction

Before:

ORIGINAL VERSION

The Last Members of the Human Race...

... Are Trapped in an Alien Zoo.

Harl Eriksson has never seen Earth. Born and raised in an alien zoo the only life he's ever known is in a small village trapped in glass.

Giant eyes peer in to the exhibit, the eyes of a nameless, oppressive being that rules over the village like a silent, cruel god.

When people begin disappearing, some tremble, some pray; Harl sharpens his axe and sets out to be his world's first cage breaker. He's got questions and he's going to get answers one way or another...

LATEST VERSION

What if you discovered your world was a zoo…

And humans were the animal on display?

The last humans in the galaxy live in a fish tank.

Trapped inside a terrarium world, a single alien provides the remaining humans with everything we need to survive, everything except our freedom.

When the "God" reaches inside, the hand of providence steals away our loved ones and leaves a trail of destruction in its wake.

Harl Eriksson refuses to worship the so-called god and vows to kill the giant on the other side of the glass.

He swears vengeance on the creature that stole his parents and in a twist of fate finds himself on the outside of the impenetrable tank wall.

But how to destroy a thousand foot alien god?

Delve into the Humanarium today for an adventure you won't be able to put down.

Get it now.

Analysis:

He made two attempts. His plan was to test them both. I stepped in before he spent much time testing what I believe are sub-par descriptions. It was better to get Chris on the right track without the wasted effort.

I see what he's trying to do with the hooks, but it just doesn't make me want to read any further. The core concept makes me think there might be a good story here, but Chris has focused on the wrong things. The "Humans in a Zoo" just isn't intriguing enough, and it sort of gives away everything.

In the second one, he gives away that the hero someone gets out of the zoo by a twist of fate. There are just too many spoilers.

He gets points for trying to bring the reader into the description with the "Delve into…" line. It's not as strong as using "You'll" and "Because," but he does get a "you" in there. So that's not bad.

Let's see if we can do better.

Meeks Version:

It stole his parents.

Now, he's trapped in the "village."

Will no one join him and fight?

Harl's life has been limited to the small village he shares with strangers. He doesn't know how he got there. There doesn't seem to be a way to leave. His captors demand he worship their god. If he doesn't give in, it could mean his life.

How much is freedom worth?

The captors are cruel, though they provide what is needed to survive. Living each day not knowing what comes next is the worst sort of torture. And remembering the death of his parents at the hand of "their" god haunts him.

The aliens call it a zoo.

The humans need a hero.

But will it be enough?

You'll love this amazing adventure, because everyone enjoys a fight for the survival of the human race against all odds.

Get it now.

Analysis:

I played down the zoo stuff. It's part of the story, and an important part, but I believe the details should be a surprise for the readers once they begin the journey.

And do we need all the specifics about the thousand-foot god? No. I believe that tidbit is best left for the book, not the description.

I especially like the second line, with the village in quotes. Just that alone is intriguing to me. What does it mean?

The next line includes more intrigue.

Throughout my version, I just hint at the story. It's a stronger description.

IMPORTANT:
POST-TESTING REPORT

I was wrong!

Chris was great. He sent me data once per week and we compared his numbers, and in the end, the description I had written, the one I was *sure* was an improvement, did not beat his Blurb Two.

He had used the methodology I taught in my course and done a fine job. I just didn't give his blurb the credit it deserved.

We watched the data for 60 days. He had limited data on the second blurb, so when we both were not happy with the conversion rate on mine, we decided to switch to blurb two, and it outperformed.

THIS IS CRUCIAL TO UNDERSTAND:
NO SINGLE OPINION IS AS GOOD AS ACTUAL DATA.

I wrote a description that seemed stronger to me because the whole zoo thing turned me off, but I am not his readers. They liked the zoo bit. The data showed they preferred his hooks to mine. Does that mean that his description is now as good as it can be?

Nope.

It just means that of the three we've tried, we've found the best performer. There is always room for improvement. And the only way to find out if a change is resulting in better conversions is to take the time to gather the data and then to do the math.

CHAPTER TWENTY-FOUR

Description Twelve - Fantasy

Author: Yvette Bostic
Title: *Light's Rise (Light in the Darkness Book 1)*
Price: $3.99
Genre: Fantasy

Before:

Original Version

Darian was a young scout in the Imperial Austrian Army when Napoleon Bonaparte started his campaign across Europe. When Darian witnesses the people of his hometown being led to their deaths by enormous horned creatures, he realizes that Europe's war is dwarfed by an even greater threat.

A mysterious man named Raphael provides Darian with two choices: stay and fight against the French, or join the Council of Light in the struggle to save Europe from a demonic overlord intent on conquering humanity.

Darian's choice leads him into a new war, where victory lies in the hands of an unusual group of warriors with supernatural abilities whose sole purpose is to protect them all from an unending tide of evil.

LATEST VERSION

Demons are being summoned from hell.

Darian, a scout in the Imperial Austrian Army, witnesses the people of his hometown being led to their deaths by enormous horned creatures.

The war that is raging across Europe, thanks to Napoleon, has been dwarfed by this humanity-devouring threat. A man named Raphael provides Darian with two choices: stay and fight against the French, or join the Council of Light in the struggle to save Europe from a demonic overlord intent on destroying humanity.

Darian's choice leads him to an evil place, where humans are sacrificed and his only hope is a band of warriors with supernatural abilities.

Will Zar'Asur, the demon overlord, succeed in his plans or will Darian find a way to stop him before it's too late?

Analysis:

Here we have the original blurb and a revised edition. The first attempt is pretty typical of what we mostly see from authors. It's mostly just a straightforward synopsis.

The second one is better, but not by much. There is an attempt at a hook. Then it goes into a synopsis, but it does finish with a hook-like question, so that's an improvement.

Let's see if we can do better.

Meeks Version:

Who summoned the beasts?

Darian knows only one thing…

…they're from hell and must be stopped.

The Napoleonic Wars rage. Darian is a scout for the Imperial Austrian army, and he's just met the strangest of men. If he hadn't seen the demons himself, he wouldn't believe Raphael.

But Raphael knows a secret.

And Darian must make a choice. The French must be stopped. Yet the demons he's seen make his blood run cold. Could it be true? Is there a demonic overlord planning to wipe out humanity?

How does one choose between two wars, when either could destroy all he loves?

You'll love this alternative history fantasy because of the depth and realism to the journey.

Get it now.

Analysis:

What I really like are the parts "strangest of men" and "Raphael knows a secret." For me, I want to know why he's so strange. It paints an enthralling visual image… and I also want to know, what *is* his secret?

CHAPTER TWENTY-FIVE

ARTICLE - SHE SOMETIMES FEELS BAD

She sometimes feels bad...

...and beats herself up.

An indie author like most of us, but she doesn't see what makes her special.

She doesn't know why she's NOT like most of us, she's better.

This woman has written 25 books. That's more than I've written. That's more than a lot of people have written. It's not more than our founder, Michael Anderle, or his partner in crime, Craig Martelle, have written, but I bet they would agree that this next story is incredible.

Even they may be impressed.

This woman has, over the last 18 months or so, asked me for advice or thoughts on this business. It's my pleasure to help when I can.

I didn't know that she has a two-year-old. That means that at one point, she had a six-month-old who was being an infant 24/7 and continued to grow into a toddler (the most dangerous of the child age groups), all while she was working on her business.

That increases the difficulty score considerably.

Even the Russian judges are impressed.

This was NOT the story.

You see, she came to me tonight with a question about keywords. I told her a bit about the research I've done and stopped her from panicking with her own test.

She mentioned that she's been tired.

I asked why.

Her answer made me take a deep breath.

I'm not a parent. Parenting scares me.

She's just had another baby.

And when she began writing for Nano month, the newborn was just under four weeks old.

I'm sure the moms can imagine what her life was (and is) like right now.

She's written 30,000 words thus far.

That's more than I've written this month.

It's probably less than Michael Anderle and Craig Martelle have written, but again, she gets bonus points for the difficulty level.

And I don't mean just having a baby to keep alive.

She's written 30,000 words...

...on her phone...

...with her thumb, while the kid sleeps in her other arm.

We're all dedicated to our businesses, but this is some next level stuff.

I can't imagine writing with my thumb... or even holding a baby... but to do both at the same time? Incredible.

FULL CREDIT PUBLISHING

Do you take the time to celebrate what you've overcome to get here?

Just getting through the first book is amazing.

Nobody lives in a vacuum. And you need to understand that for some of us, who have had the good fortune to find a little success and can do this full-time, we've got it easier than a lot of you.

And YOU need to give yourself credit each time you find 10 minutes on a lunch break to write words.

Or set the alarm a little earlier for one more chapter.

It's a long road.

You'll find the journey a bit less fraught with self-doubt if you pay attention to the things you're doing right.

Most people don't write that first book...

...most don't have our desire.

You're here.

That means you're NOT like most people.

What's the challenge that you've overcome?

I'm sure the Russian judges will be impressed.

CHAPTER TWENTY-SIX

DESCRIPTION THIRTEEN - CONTEMPORARY WESTERN ROMANCE

Author: Stephanie Berget
Title: *Rocky Road Home*
Price: $4.99
Genre: Contemporary Western Romance

Before:

With a Harley and a ponytail, he's certainly no cowboy...

When Sissy Leviny realizes a cowboy, even if he's a champion, won't fix her life, she swears off men. Proving she's more than a party girl to her judgmental hometown is something she'll have to achieve on her own. But when a hot biker saves her from Red Whiskers and his derelict friends, she realizes that cowboys are not the only men to be trusted.

Rocky Wade left Texas for Seattle to work as a mechanic, and to escape betrayal and a broken heart. He hadn't planned on dealing with a gang of rednecks or the freak snowstorm that strands him with a dead-set-against-men, blonde spitfire. As the snow melts so does Rocky's pain, but can he chance giving his heart again?

Can Sissy change her ideal vision of a man from one that rides horses and wears a Stetson, to one who has a ponytail and prefers the roar of a Harley?

Opposites attract in this contemporary western romance where the look of love isn't always what you'd envisioned.

Analysis:

By this point, I'm sure you see what I do. It's too much synopsis and not enough hook. For my version, I took out everything about the story and just wrote a pure copywriting piece designed to grab the reader by the belt buckle and not let go.

Meeks Version:

That ain't no cowboy.

So why was she still checking him out?

The rumble of the Harley drowned out the radio in her truck. George Strait sang about Amarillo, and she just stared. The light seemed to stay red forever, or maybe time had stopped. Why didn't his ponytail and leather jacket bother her? Maybe it was those cheekbones?

He turned his head.

His chiseled chin pointed right at her and paused.

Sissy flashed her best smile, wondered if her hair was a mess, forgetting that she was wearing her Stetson. And without even knowing why, she switched on flirt mode. It was a mindset she got into when she wanted to make the cowboys fall in love with her.

Nothing.

He didn't nod.

She wondered if he'd winked and she just couldn't tell behind his sunglasses.

The light turned green, and the thundering horses of his hog took him away. Time remained stopped. She didn't hit the gas. She just kept thinking, Who was that man? And why would she care? She liked cowboys.

He was definitely not her type.

A car honked.

And time started again, but would she ever be the same?

Her story would soon begin in a way she never imagined possible.

You'll love this contemporary western romance because not everyone is what they seem.

Get it now.

Analysis:

Not every description needs to be about the book. For this one, I went with a little moment of time that isn't in the book. It doesn't matter. Though, admittedly, it would be a cool start to the story if this were the opening chapter.

The point is, readers won't remember the description; they'll just get into the story they're told.

I think of this description as a "prequel."

Did you get hooked?

CHAPTER TWENTY-SEVEN

DESCRIPTION FOURTEEN - WIZARDS AND WITCHES

Author: Thea Atkinson
Title: *Grim (Reaper's Redemption Book 1)*
Price: $4.99
Genre: Wizards and Witches

Before:

ORIGINAL VERSION

Who reaps the souls of the Supernatural?

Ayla doesn't believe in monsters.

But when a text from a friend flickers across her cell phone, all that changes.

This is Sarah, a friend from foster care who shared frightening stories of rituals and black magic. Who disappeared without a word for years...

Until now.

Now she wants to meet at an abandoned gothic cathedral. At midnight. Alone.

Except Sarah isn't there when Ayla arrives. Instead, there's a tattooed maniac muttering Latin prayers and telling her she needs to die.

That's when Ayla discovers there are worse things than monsters who want her dead.

There's the Angel of Death who wants her alive.

Grim is the first installment of the hot new Reaper's Redemption series, an urban fantasy collection with supernatural creatures of all kinds. If you enjoy clean but romantic stories with supernatural beings and heroes in unexpected places, you will want to pick up your copy of Grim.

PICK IT UP today and find out if you believe in monsters.

Analysis:

Thea's starting point was okay. It's not too heavy on the paragraphs. There are hooks, though I think they could be better. The CTA is a little long. Also, I don't think the lengthy paragraph about it being part of the Reaper's Redemption series is especially good copywriting.

I had her try a new one after we talked.

SECOND VERSION

There are worse things than monsters...

There are angels.

Ayla doesn't believe in supernatural creatures. But when a text from a long-lost friend flickers across her cell phone, all that changes.

This is Sarah, a friend from foster care who shared frightening stories of rituals and black magic. A friend who disappeared without a word for years...

Until now.

And she wants to meet at an abandoned Gothic cathedral.

At midnight.

Alone.

Now Ayla is about to discover that the only thing worse than making a deal with the devil is to make one with an angel.

Grim is the first installment of the urban fantasy series, Reaper's Redemption. If you love stories with supernatural creatures and heroes in unexpected places you will want to pick up your copy of Grim.

PICK IT UP today and find out if you believe in monsters.

Analysis:

This is an improvement. The opening hook is intriguing. It makes me want to know how angels are worse than monsters. The middle section is also really solid and pulls the reader through to the ending. She also improved on the last paragraph about its place in the series.

Meeks Version:

Her life is about to change.

All because of a single text.

Where has Sarah been all these years?

Sarah was her best friend. They went way back. Ayla has always adored her, even if she never understood Sarah's interest in black magic. Then one day she was gone without a word.

When the text message from Sarah asks her to meet, Ayla has no idea what she's about to get into. She just goes, wondering why Sarah is hiding out in a church.

In that abandoned gothic cathedral…

…Ayla learns a secret.

There's something worse than monsters. But she's a skeptic. She doesn't believe in monsters or angels.

Will it get her killed?

You'll adore this Urban Fantasy because of the twists and turns. It's tough to put down.

Get it now.

Analysis:

My version is a slight improvement over her second attempt. I like the hook a little bit more. The final paragraph about the genre is tightened up a tad. And the call-to-action is short.

Yes, I do ONLY use "Get it now." That may be annoying, but it's simple, and that's what we're going for.

The point of this third version is that one can write a really good description and it might still have a little room for improvement. Never assume you've just written the last description for the book you're working on.

You may be a better copywriter in a year, or you might attack it from a different perspective.

CHAPTER TWENTY-EIGHT

DESCRIPTION FIFTEEN - NEW ADULT & COLLEGE

Author: Logan Byrne (not related to my pen name Arthur Byrne)
Title: *Awakened Spells (Awakened Spells Book One)*
Price: $2.99
Genre: New Adult & College, Werewolves & Shifters

Before:

ORIGINAL VERSION

When you're a thief trying to get by on the scraps of your labor, life is anything but easy.

Lexa Blackmoon, orphan and low-end magical thief, is just trying to get by the best way she can. But when a shadow mage tells her she's meant for something greater, she can't help feeling he's telling the truth.

Taken to a secret resistance camp, Lexa learns that not only is she a mage, but she bears the Mark of Merlin, a magical power greater than she's ever dreamt of. She trains her powers to infiltrate the ranks of the magical police force tasked with keeping the arcane realm secret from normal humans.

But when the sinister president-turned-dictator, Kiren Nightstorm, attempts to take over the realm, Lexa must defeat his secret crime syndicate before he enslaves the entire magical race.

This book features a strong witch heroine and fast-paced action and adventure, including werewolves, shifters, vampires, and more!

SECOND VERSION

The magical and mortal realms are under attack. A rune mage seeks to destroy us all.

An orphan thief, my powers stayed dormant until a man came to me from the shadows.

He gave me a wand, the resistance teaching me and harboring my newly growing powers.

They paired me with mages and shifters; together we need to infiltrate the magical police force to stop him.

The problem? He controls their top brass, and they can't know our people are infiltrating their ranks.

This book features a strong witch heroine and fast-paced action and adventure, including werewolves, shifters, vampires, and more!

Analysis:

Neither one of these hooks me. The newest is just a list. Its formatting isn't good. It just doesn't invite the potential reader to want to bother reading the description.

Meeks Version:

Lexa is hungry.

Will her meager magical skill let her survive another day?

In a world of shifters, vampires, werewolves, and mages, the nighttime can be scary. For Lexa, life as a thief is hard. Living as an orphan makes it worse. Lexa knows adults can't be trusted. She's been lied to before. So why should she believe the Shadow Mage who says she's meant for greater things?

In the darkness, trouble looms. Lexa can't sense it, yet, but others are talking. They speak of a rune mage. Are the rumors true?

She must make a choice.

If there is a battle coming, Lexa must take a side, but more than that, she must learn her craft. The werewolves and shifters are preparing. The time is now.

It may be the only thing that keeps her alive.

You'll love this vampire and shifter adventure, because everyone enjoys a fight for survival.

Get it now.

Analysis:

Nothing earth-shattering here. I worked in the main genre themes and included some hints at what might be in the story.

Also, I really don't care for first person... and he wrote in first person. That had to go.

CHAPTER TWENTY-NINE

And they gathered...

The authors, editors, dreamers, and poets, all in one place...

...to meet and greet and sometimes hug.

I'm pro-hug.

Craig Martelle asked a question the other day, "What is your one thing?"

Meaning, what was the one thing you took away from last year that stood out?

Last year, for me, it was the energy. We're like Tesla batteries, and when put in a room together for a few days, we charge up to max capacity.

When it ends, we're exhausted, but a good night's sleep (or three) and we're ready to start using that fuel.

My year since the last convention has been a good one. I did fuel up at Bryan Cohen's convention in Chicago, and it got me through to tonight.

Is there a point to your rambling, Brian?

Maybe...

Okay, yes.

In this profession, we have ample opportunities to attend these sorts of gatherings. Many attend, but most do not.

This post is for those of you who aren't sure if there is value.

THERE IS LOTS OF VALUE.

The list of takeaways is longer than a CVS receipt for three items. (If you've not been to CVS then the length of their register tape is enough to reach from southern California to Narnia and back.)

I digress...

The point is, each person leaves with knowledge or motivation and usually both.

The new authors see what's possible…

…the seasoned writers find new inspiration.

At dinner tonight, there were four folks I got to talk to a bunch, and I loved it.

One of them, though, was staggeringly impressive in her work ethic.

She was not an author; she's an editor (and fully booked, so don't ask who it was), and her output per month (qty. of books edited) was a number that I didn't think was possible.

I'm not often surprised.

It was the sort of number that humbles one and lifts them up.

I can do better, I thought.

Look at what she gets done.

I love meeting extraordinary people, and I got to do that tonight many times over.

The volume of things I want to do always dwarfs the volume I get done, but that's okay. I don't want to ever feel too caught up. The race is part of the fun.

But what if I changed a few things?

What if I got a little more organized?

What is possible then?

To those who are not here in Las Vegas this week, we shall miss you. Perhaps next year you'll be able to come?

Maybe you'll find another gathering to attend?

If you have any doubts on the value, though, put those thoughts aside, because you will become richer for the experience.

You WILL learn something.

You WILL have fun.

Now that's all I have for tonight. Thanks to everyone I got to talk to this evening. You were delightful.

CHAPTER THIRTY

Author: Angus McLean
Title: *Old Friends*
Price: Free
Genre: Hard-Boiled Detective

Before:

Tough Auckland private eye Dan Crowley faces off against a gang of murderous thugs when he is called on to help out his old mate, Mike Manning.

A trucking firm faces collapse from unexplained stock thefts and Mike's reputation and freedom are on the line when he stands accused. He brings in his old mate Dan, proprietor of Chase Investigations, to clear his name and catch the real culprits. Backed up by Dan's resourceful wife Molly they investigate further and try to keep one step ahead of his long-standing nemesis, DI Kennedy, but the boys are up against it to close the case unscathed and with their friendship intact.

Analysis:

Typically, I'd write something snarky here, but this one is EXTREMELY similar to ALL the descriptions I used to write before I studied copywriting, so it hits a little close to home.

Man... back in the day I just hated writing them so much. I have no idea if Angus put a lot of thought into this or not, but I know I never did. I just wrote a brief bit about the book and was glad to be done with it.

We can do better.

Meeks Version:

Dan's been in tough spots.

It comes with being a private eye.

This time, he may be in over his head.

His old mate is in trouble, standing accused of theft. Stock is being stolen from a local trucking firm. If Dan can't help a friend in need, then what's the point of even getting into this racket?

There's just one problem.

As he starts to dig, feathers get ruffled.

People with thick necks and poor dispositions don't appreciate Dan's digging around. They've made it clear he should mind his own business.

Loyalty is important, but will it get him killed?

You'll love this gritty, hard-boiled detective story, because the author, Angus McLean, is a real police detective who knows how to craft a story to keep you guessing.

Get it now.

Analysis:

I like some of the visuals here. The line about "people with thick necks" really speaks to the genre. Also, in my "You'll…because" section, I went a different way. Angus really is a police detective.

In fact, when I offered to write this description for him (and the book), he was going to bed because he had to get up early to work on a homicide investigation.

The fact that he's got some credentials will really play well with the audience he's trying to serve.

This won't necessarily be the case for all genres. If you write fantasy, and you're a high-level wizard, then you should use it. If you're a romance writer and have had sex—well, that may not be worth mentioning.

You get the point.

CHAPTER THIRTY-ONE

Description Seventeen - Paranormal, Occult & Supernatural

Author: Miranda Hardy and Jay Noel
Title: *Death Knocks (Black-Eyed Kids Book 1)*
Price: $3.99
Genre: Paranormal, Occult & Supernatural

Before:

Who knew a knock at the door could tear your world apart? They don't demand money or possessions…they want much more than that, they want your life.

Maverick is preparing for senior year: he's no longer stuck in the "friend-zone" with the girl of his dreams, he's looking forward to choosing the right college and being on his own, and he plans to have a blast along the way.

But a knock on the door changes all of that forever.

Maverick begins a mind-altering, life-changing journey to discover the truth—a truth that certain individuals will do anything to keep hidden.

Analysis:

This is good copywriting… actually, no. This is GREAT copywriting. It just needs some formatting and a couple of tweaks.

Meeks Version:

Who knew a knock at the door would tear their world apart?

The Black-Eyed Kids don't demand money…

…they want more than that. They want Maverick's life.

Maverick is preparing for senior year: he's no longer stuck in the "friend-zone" with Lisa, the girl of his dreams. He's looking forward to college and being on his own. The plan is to have a blast along the way.

A knock on the door changes his life forever.

Maverick is taken on a mind-altering, life-changing journey to discover the truth—a truth that the "Kids" will do anything to keep hidden.

You'll love this fast-paced YA Paranormal Thriller, because everyone enjoys a battle against evil.

Get it now.

Analysis:

I changed a few things. Can you spot them?

In the first line, we changed "could" to "would." We felt it had more of a pending doom feel. Also, we changed "your" to "their."

"Your" makes it feel like the description includes the reader in the story, but it isn't the reader's life that is torn apart; it's Maverick's and Lisa's lives that are in trouble.

The rest of my tiny changes should make the writing a little shorter and tighter. Make no mistake, the copy was entirely Miranda's and was brilliant.

CHAPTER THIRTY-TWO

Description Eighteen - LGBTQ Paranormal Romance

Author: Patricia D. Eddy
Title: *Destined*
Price: $3.99
Genre: Paranormal Romance, LGBTQ Romance

Before:

Broken. Afraid. Alone.

Ami fears she'll never feel safe again. Never be free from her nightmares of the time she spent as the Clan Kendrick's prisoner.

Until, Seònaid, her true mate shows up at Raven and Ealasaid's door. The quiet witch comforts Ami, even as she harbors a dark secret.

When Seònaid admits the truth, will Ami run from the one woman who can heal her scars? Or can magic—and love—save both of them?

Analysis:

Too much information-dump and not enough hook.
But we can remedy that.

Meeks Version:

Ami's greatest fear.

Will she always be alone?

A quiet witch enters her life. She's got powers beyond belief. This witch knows things Ami has never dreamed of, but will she share?

Ami senses there's more to this woman. She's right. Will Ami run from the one woman who can heal her scars? Or can magic—and love—save them? The witch has a dark secret that can destroy them. Will they be able to build a life together?

You'll adore this take on lesbian romance, because love is love.

Get it now.

Analysis:

The opening hook is similar to the original, but instead of just listing facts, we took them and asked a question. It's a question many potential readers may have asked themselves.

This is a good hook.

CHAPTER THIRTY-THREE

Is it time to quit?

I've seen that question before.

It always makes me sad. We all know this business can be tough. We all have had days where lack of progress broke our hearts. And for some...

...the voice of doubt can creep into their minds.

Don't let it.

There's never a time to quit.

If you're writing, you're winning.

This game doesn't have a shot clock. It's not a race. It's not a competition.

In fact, it's not even a single game. It's a unique game we all play with our own set of rules.

THE PROBLEM...

...comparison.

You have every right to look at authors who are crushing it and be inspired.

You are NOT allowed to feel bad about yourself because your numbers are less impressive.

Their life is not your life.

Maybe they're a middle-aged, short, balding, guy WITHOUT kids, who does the author thing full-time, and who doesn't have much of his day eaten up by supermodels wanting to go on dates.

Maybe YOU have kids, a job, a social life that's important, and can only devote 30 minutes per day to this business.

40 to 80 available work hours per week shouldn't be compared to 3.5.

But that's not the only thing.

This business requires a lot of learning. Some authors come to the table with skillsets that mean they don't need to learn some of the stuff.

A former copywriter will be able to master the marketing side more quickly than someone who knows nothing about the art.

A person who built Excel workbooks as their job will have skills that a neophyte to Excel will have to learn.

Maybe they know analytics…

…maybe you need to Google what variance means and how it's important.

Maybe THEY have been at this longer.

The point is, Indies Authors are awesome. We're happy to help. And given enough time, you can succeed at this business.

The hardest part is writing that first book.

98% of the world THINKS about writing a book.

YOU have already overcome that hurdle.

YOU are already winning.

Now you just need to eat some chocolate and give yourself a break.

You're doing great.

CHAPTER THIRTY-FOUR

Author: Lina Langley
Title: *Boy + Friend*
Price: $5.99
Genre: LGBTQ Anthologies and Collections

Before:

Boy + Friend is a collection of romantic m/m stories by bestselling author Lina Langley. They're friends. Friendship is great... but these men are feeling a different type of love.
    Stories include:
    - Promises of Eternity
    When Gabriel's best friend Holden gets left at the altar, Gabriel has to step up his emotional support. It doesn't take long for him to realize what his true feelings are toward Holden.
    - Be Mine
    Mac Adler has had a crush on his best friend Barrett for the longest time. Kissing him should be a good thing, except it might have destroyed their friendship for good. Mac isn't sure how to fix it.
    - Chasing The Sea
    It's just Hunter, the guy he's interested in, a cat and a boat... It's the perfect opportunity to make a move. That's until they need to take the boat

back in and Hunter realizes he's going to have to pick between who he wants to be with and his family.

- A La Carte Friend

For most best friends, becoming stepbrothers would be a dream come true. For anyone else, it would be easy, but Brighton's crush on his new stepbrother is getting too hard to handle. Especially when it's clear Jaden feels the same way,

Switch

- Greg knows he shouldn't keep secrets from his best friend, especially not about his sexuality. But Kyle has secrets of his own. Can their secrets bring them closer together or will they tear them apart for good?

Warning: This story may contain triggering content. It is approximately 100,000+ words in length and contains language & erotic adult scenes. It is intended for adults.

Analysis:

This sort of description is pretty common for an anthology. The little bits for each book were fine. It's all pretty much by the numbers, but I don't think those numbers add up to sales.

Meeks Version:

Friendship matters.

But what if it could be more?

Who will take the risk to find out?

Traversing the gay dating world can be an emotional mind-blower. There's much to consider, and these guys, in their respective stories, have complicated lives that make finding love anything but easy.

Is amazing sex worth the emotional risk?

These steamy tales look beyond the bedroom and into the lives of these ten men. The drama is real. Will their lives change for the better, or will a first move ruin everything?

You'll enjoy the tapestry of their worlds, because we all—gay or straight—

have experienced the crushing self-doubt that makes finding love the greatest challenge in life.

Get it now.

Analysis:

I took a more global view of the book. Instead of summing up what happens in each story, I let the potential reader know that it's a collection of lives with different struggles.

Each of us has been through the wringer with a crush and can relate. It's my hope to entice readers beyond just the gay community who are interested in a good collection of stories.

The warning she put in the end about the sex, I covered in not so many words.

I removed the "Trigger Warning" because there is an increasingly vocal subset of the politically correct community which now believes that the word is overused and thus has cheapened the meaning for people who suffer from mental illness.

I don't know if this is true or not. Please don't be triggered. It's just best to leave it out as it may become a no-win sort of word.

CHAPTER THIRTY-FIVE

Author: Jeremy Fabiano
Title: *Legend of the Sword Bearer*
Price: $4.99
Genre: LitRPG/Fantasy

Before:

Life after death can be heaven—or hell…

His body ravaged by a fatal illness, Steve is offered a deal he can't refuse: to have his consciousness transferred into an exclusive RPG. He takes on his newfound persona, a warrior named Abalonious. But a malevolent in-game force puts much more than Abalonious's game world at stake…

If Abalonious is to survive, he must discover this world's crucial secrets in time to stop the darkness from enslaving the souls of Tempest and turning Abalonious's afterlife into a digital hell.

Legend of the Sword Bearer is the first book in a new LitRPG series. If you like nerdy fantasy heroes, pop culture references, epic battles, and immersive gaming worlds, then you'll love Jeremy Fabiano's Tempest Chronicles.

Buy Legend of the Sword Bearer and join the battle for Tempest today!

Analysis:

It's pretty solid. I like the premise, but I wonder if it can be done in a way that isn't, "so here's what happens."

I also like the last paragraph, but I don't care for the CTA. It's too long. We need to be able to see it without reading it. Short and to the point.

Meeks Version:

Steve's days are numbered.

The illness has consumed him.

Would this stranger's offer give him a second chance?

It looks like a game. Looks can be deceiving. Paul Nelson, the CEO of Tempest Inc., has developed another world, and he's ready to send in another consciousness. This time, though, things are different. Those that came before have caused some troubles, and his world is in peril.

For Steve, it's a last chance. He's got nothing to lose. And who knows, it might be fun?

As a warrior named Abalonious and with his physical body gone, Steve must adapt, learn, and grow to survive. But this world isn't exactly as advertised. There's a darkness coming. It looks like fun will have to wait.

And there's a secret nobody wants to talk about.

Will Steve piece together enough to live?

If you like nerdy fantasy heroes, pop culture references, epic battles, and immersive gaming worlds, then you'll love this adventure.

Get it now.

Analysis:

My version is not vastly different from the original. I took out some of the specific details and try to add a little more hook to it. I did add in a little more detail about how Steve gets into the world.

Generally, I don't want to add a synopsis, but it seemed needed to bring it all together so it would make sense.

Here's another thing I felt was important: I eliminated a bunch of the instances of the warrior's name. It's long, and it's not easy to read, so I stuck with "Steve."

Also, I didn't include the bit about saving the world. It's rather cliché. Of course, we all love reading those stories, but I'm not sure it adds to the copy.

CHAPTER THIRTY-SIX

ARTICLE - DON'T BELIEVE THE LIES

Don't believe the lies...

There's a myth in this business, and it's killing you (Smalls).

It's the single piece of advice I hear given that makes me want to go on a tri-state killing spree, while screaming at the top of my lungs and blasting the sound of fingernails on chalkboards over an industrial-sized speaker system.

And I'm a pacifist.

"Do what the successful authors in your genre are doing."

This phrase is the equivalent to unleashing gerbils during the age of the Black Death (Note: from 1347 the Black Death, Bubonic Plague, ravaged Europe for 400 years. It had been blamed on rats until recently when it was determined they had been framed... by gerbils. I digress.)

The point is, this is the most dangerous advice given because it makes so much sense.

But the flawed logic is crushing MOST authors' revenue.

There are three areas where this advice gets bandied about:

1) Cover Art
2) Pricing
3) Descriptions

The good news is, the advice 100% makes sense for cover art. The top sellers generally have GREAT covers. Do what they do, and you'll have GREAT covers, too.

It's the next two that are a problem.

A big problem.

Are you ready for the truth?
You can't handle the truth!!!

———

Before I get into specifics, I want to talk about the global impact of this falsehood.

We (indie authors) are a massive force in the industry.

Our success is the inspiration that convinces those on the sidelines to give writing a book a try.

We will change the lives of people who don't even know they want to become authors.

That's pretty cool.

But also, if we collectively do something bad, can, without meaning to, hurt everyone.

This is why I'm writing this post.

It's time we turn up our game for future generations of Indie Authors.

———

Let's look at pricing.

Imagine an author who has a five-book series, priced at 99 cents for book 1 and $2.99 for books 2 - 5.

Note: There are absolutely cases where a 99-cent first book (or even FREE) makes sense. THIS IS NOT suggesting that those are bad ideas for some, but the number of authors for which this makes sense is a tiny fraction of those who do it.

This author is considering raising her price on book 1.

She's afraid her ranking will drop.

This is the first problem.

It's a massive issue.

**************** IMPORTANT *****************

It's okay if your ranking drops.

It matters WAY less than you think because you can drive your ranking back up with advertising.

My best ranking for *Underwood, Scotch, and Wry* was #520 - #980 overall for 10 days, TWO YEARS after it was released.

DO NOT LET THIS FEAR RUIN YOUR BUSINESS.

*************** End of Mini Rant ***************

Her fear of ranking drop SHOULD be replaced with a fear of missed opportunity.

Let me give an example.

An author is making $4,000 per month on $1,200 ad spend. He has followed the horrible advice and has his books priced like the top sellers, his description is similar, and his back matter is nearly identical.

In short, he's doing it ALL FREAKING WRONG.

After 3 months of rewriting all his descriptions. Raising his price to FULL-PRICE (which I consider to be $4.99) and fixing his back matter...

...he is making $7,000 per month on ZERO ad spend.

Yes, we killed 100% of his ads because they were NOT helping.

So, he went from $2,800 in Net Profit to $7,000 in net profit.

He is NO longer following the horrible gerbil-plague-ridden advice.

And you know what happened last month? Well, he had $25,000 in sales on $9,000 ad spend.

So, now he's up to $16,000 net profit.

Question for people afraid of math...

Which is better: $16,000 in profit or $2,800?

Let's go back to our example.

The author in question is afraid of losing a few sales and a few ranking points.

Why isn't she afraid of LOSING the potential to make 5 TIMES what she does now?

I want you to think about that.

By NOT testing new properly written descriptions and prices, YOU are risking substantial growth in your business.

Now think about how that impacts the next 20 years of your life.

With my client mentioned above, if we NEVER improve again (which we will, because I'm really good at this stuff), we're talking about a difference of 4.7 million dollars over 20 years.

That's a BIG penalty for "doing what the successful people are doing."

Are you afraid of what you're missing?

Good!

Question from the minds of the readers:

"But Brian, how are they making so much money if they're doing it wrong?"

Answer: In the world of the blind, the one-eyed man is King.

It's a level playing field. EVERYONE is doing it wrong. They are the top performers because they write good books and have built a following.

But how much are they leaving on the table?

They may never know because of the same fear this author has.

———

So, back to our 5-book author.

What should she do?

The first step is to learn proper copywriting. (Note: That's why you're reading this book.)

Then she should raise her prices to $4.99 across all 5 books.

"But Brian, everyone in my genre prices at..."

Stop it! Go back to the beginning and reread the post up to this point.

———

The case for $4.99.

My degree is in Economics.

The Theory of Price Elasticity of Demand is from Econ 101.

Please stop eye-rolling and keep reading. It's important.

The basic gist of it is that if the price of a product is elastic, then the most profitable move is to lower the price.

The lower the price (up to a point), the higher the volume of sales, and that higher volume is SO LARGE that the total profit is greater even with a smaller margin.

Amazon books—and I've studied hundreds of authors' data—are NOT price-elastic!!!

They are price inelastic.

This is the opposite. The increase in price may lead to a slight decrease in sales, but the additional revenue is greater.

In short, people don't really care if they're paying $2.99 or $4.99 when they pay 5 bucks EVERY SINGLE DAY of the year for a coffee from Starbucks that they drink in 15 minutes.

But the price inelasticity point is NOT the only benefit.

There's one more.

And I've studied this, too.

You will convert MORE KU subscribers and get them to download your book because of PERCEIVED value at the higher price.

AND... your boxed sets will do better, too.

————

So this author needs to raise her prices.

AND she needs to watch the numbers for a month.

AND she needs to CORRECTLY analyze her data.

This means she needs to NOT just look at the bottom line, but also consider the number of clicks.

She can't raise the price and compare her numbers to the previous month WITHOUT also knowing the number of paid clicks she had.

If July was 4,884 clicks and August, when she made the change, is only 2211 clicks, she MUST do some math to figure out which one was superior.

————

Conclusions:

I want you to consider how much you're killing your business by not running a test of higher prices.

It's a big deal.

But it's also a big deal to OUR entire Indie Publishing Industry.

I might get 500 - 700 people to read a post like this in the 20books group.

That's a small portion of the 28,000+ who are members.

And I'll likely post it to my group, too, and get a few hundred more.

But what if 500 people raised their prices?

What if, next month, there was a flood of posts saying, "I raised my prices, and it was good. Thanks, Brian Meeks, for making the suggestion. May I introduce you to my 44-year-old, single, former swimsuit model sister who loves golf?"

Well, how many people would those posts reach?

How long would it take before $4.99 truly was the standard?

How much weight would I lose trying to impress the 44-year old single golfer?

We can change the industry.

Not by FORCING higher prices but by CORRECTLY pricing our books.

And I really could stand to lose a few pounds.

Thanks for reading.

What will YOUR numbers look like next month?

(Note: The book I pictured with this when I posted it originally is priced at $9.99 and has ZERO advertising. It's been out for 54 weeks. I suspect that 100% of the authors in this group would have NOT priced it at $9.99 because it's only 44,000 words, but I assessed the value of the book and believed it would do just fine.

Over a year later, it is still selling.

Always test and analyze your data. It matters.)

P.s. Did you get to this point?

That's almost 1,500 words in a FB post. That's a freaking lot of words.

Do you know WHY you read the whole monstrous thing?

It's written with proper copywriting. There are hooks, small paragraphs, and I kept you sucked in.

Remember that. It will help you.

Thanks again.

CHAPTER THIRTY-SEVEN

Copywriting for Dating - Sarah Noffke

This is a Bumble Dating Bio for my friend and author, Sarah Noffke. It should be noted this was written while in Bali at the 20BooksBali conference, there had been drinking, and Sarah doesn't really need a dating profile as she is super freaking awesome, but she let me do it anyway.

Also, her daughter Lydia had bullied me into going down the water slide earlier in the day, which was a blast. So, this quote is really from her. Until you've been bullied by a seven-year-old, you've not really lived.

Meeks Version:

"Greatest Mom Ever" - Lydia

Short and snarky with a side order of awesome.

I'm a novelist. I love sci-fi. And I have a cat, who may or may not be bent on world domination.

Yes, I'm really smart, have a good job, and am great at making you think you're the Alpha so as not to hurt your fragile male ego.

Swipe right now.

CHAPTER THIRTY-EIGHT

Description Twenty-One - Steampunk

Author: Ira Robinson
Title: *Clockwork Heart: Tales of Center*
Price: $2.99
Genre: Steampunk

Before:

Action! Adventure! Humor! ... Steampunk?

If you were given the chance to live forever, would you take it? What if the offer came from an unlicensed Wizard?

Within the walls of the sprawling metropolis, Center, anything is possible. Need a dragon to do your dirty work? There's one for hire. Want to find your true love? If they're not in Center, one can be created for you.

When a man is given the offer to have his wish come true, and it only comes at the price of a few year's service, he realizes he can't pass it up.

But not everything in Center can be taken at face value...

Magic and machines, fairies and demons, humans and beings of infinite power, all call Center their home. Anything you want can be found, but sometimes what you want isn't what you need.

"Clockwork Heart, a Tale of Center, is a gripping, engaging take on the genre that will make you want more!" -- Joe L.

"This Tale of Center is a great short novelette, and I couldn't put it down." -- Rose R.

Analysis:

Not all descriptions suck. This one is pretty good.

This begs the question, what do you do if you have a better-than-average description?

Is it worth the risk to try a change?

Well, the first thing I would want to know is does the author have solid data on the existing description's conversion rate?

This is important. If you're replacing one as good as this one, then you need to have a solid understanding of what the original description converted at and not just sales.

You must know the number of downloads in KU and sales, plus you must also know your number of clicks. For authors who don't sell too much, they don't need to worry about organic sales.

But what about the ones who do get organic sales? Well, they need to dig a little deeper and try to establish a baseline with a consistent number of paid clicks (all sources) and then use some more advanced analysis techniques like moving averages to really get a feel for how the description was doing.

Once one has this figured out, then by all means, test a new one.

You'll need to let the new description have 30 - 60 days to find out if it works. If the book is an epic, well, despite what most guys will tell you, size does matter. For books over say 500 KENPC, because it takes longer for readers to finish it, you may want to go out to 60 - 90 days.

But what about the risk, Brian?

The risk is not the one you imagine. You're worried you may lose a few sales over the course of the next 30 - 60 days (or 90 for those with a really massive, thick... book). And let's assume it's worse. Then yes, you'll have lost out on sales.

But what if it's better? Or what if the try after that is better?

Then you've improved your sales and KU downloads for the next 30 years.

So the real risk is not trying.

Again, please don't just change a good description willy nilly... or Willy Wonka... or Willie Stargell for that matter. Pirates fans of a certain age will get the last reference. I digress... but I think you get my point. Power-hitting left-handers who can play first base or outfield are a huge asset when building a franchise.

Still digressing...

Let's try to make it better.

Meeks Version:

It was an offer he couldn't refuse...

...but should he?

Living forever might not be all it's cracked up to be.

Within the walls of the sprawling metropolis, Center, anything is possible. Need a dragon to do your dirty work? There's one for hire. Want to find your true love? If they're not in Center, one can be created for you.

When he got the offer, it seemed like a good deal. A couple of years' service and he comes out of it with immortality. Should he worry that the person making the proposal is an unlicensed wizard?

There are always strings.

Will these hang him?

Magic and machines, fairies and demons, humans and beings of infinite power all call Center their home. Anything you want can be found, but sometimes what you want isn't what you need.

You'll love this steampunk adventure, because it hooks you from the start.

Get it now.

Analysis:

Is this one better?

I bet if we conducted a poll, some would think so, some wouldn't. I like it, but I have an inflated sense of self-worth. The point is, it might be better, but the only way to know is to test.

You'll notice I used some of the bits from the original version verbatim. I mention this only because I wanted to use the word verbatim. This tome has been sorely lacking in Latin from the beginning.

CHAPTER THIRTY-NINE

DESCRIPTION TWENTY-TWO - NEW ADULT ROMANCE

Author: Erica Alexander
Title: *Because of Logan (Riggins U Book 1)*
Price: $3.99
Genre: New Adult Romance

Before:

All her life Skye Devereaux has been content to live in the shadow of her beautiful and vivacious fraternal twin.
But when she meets a sexy and charming police officer, Skye decides she deserves more. She's worthy of more.
Now she wants to throw off her introvert shell.
She wants to challenge her fears.
And she wants him.
So what if she's scared? She'll fake it until she makes it.

Logan Cole left behind a life he never chose to live.
Being a cop gave him the escape he needed to be on his own.
With a past he'd rather forget, he holds everyone at bay.
But when chance brings him face-to-face with an intriguing and awkward girl, Logan knows he can't let her go.
So what if he's scared?
He just needs to figure out how to let her in while protecting his heart.

Analysis:

The first line is fine writing. It sets a mood for the character. It tells us a little bit about Skye. And it is horrible copywriting.

We need a hook. And when I got to the end, there hadn't been one. I lost interest. I stopped reading.

Then I started again, because I wanted to rewrite it.

The rest is pretty tame. There just isn't a lot of meat on the bone.

Meeks Version:

She's got two problems...

Skye wants him, and she's too shy to do anything about it.

Can she get over her fears?

Living a life filled with self-doubt from living in her twin brother's shadow, she's not sure she deserves happiness. But that doesn't mean she doesn't want it. Something will have to change.

That change just might be Detective Cole.

Skye thinks there's a spark. Maybe it's just his good looks. Or perhaps she's just been alone too long. Her mind races with too many thoughts and it's messing her up. Can she find the courage to go for what she wants... love?

You'll love this New Adult romance, because we've all had to face our fears at some point.

Get it now.

Analysis:

I took out much of the background stuff and focused on one point: Skye overcoming her history and her battle to find the strength to get past it. This description should convert nicely.

Also, the formatting is much more appealing than the giant blocks of text.

CHAPTER FORTY

ARTICLE - FUEL

You may not know this…

…but you are somebody's fuel.

This business of writing and publishing is hard. We all know that. There are a lot of hours spent alone at the keyboard or alone in our head.

Some days, it takes a bit of work to get started. Some days, nothing happens at all. And maybe we feel bad…

…maybe we beat ourselves up.

Maybe we feel alone.

But then something amazing happens. We get into a chat with another author. It lifts us up.

A "you're doing great" or "thanks for your help" can give us the juice to work another day on something we love.

Because even though we love it, that doesn't mean it's not hard.

There will always be questions. We'll always have more to do than we can get done. The characters in our head will never cease to chatter away about all the things they want to do.

That's okay.

We don't have a shot clock.

We only have this game, and it goes on until we quit.

Don't quit.

Keep writing. Keep learning. And keep moving forward.

And if you see an author by the side of the road, tears running down their face, a broken quill in their hand, stop and give them a hug.

It just might get them through the next mile.

Thanks to everyone who has been my fuel. I love this community of authors. I couldn't do it without you.

Now I'm going back to work.

CHAPTER FORTY-ONE

Author: Jon Evans
Title: *Thieftaker (The Edrin Loft Mysteries Book 1)*
Price: $2.99
Genre: Fantasy and Mystery

Before:

Why was the murder of a local merchant so vicious?

Mere days after he takes charge of the Old Gate Watch House, Captain Edrin Loft must solve a crime so shocking that even veteran Sergeant Aliria Gurnt finds it stomach turning. With no witnesses or apparent motive for the crime, finding the culprit seems an impossible task.

But Loft has new scientific methods to apply to crime fighting. His first successful investigation caused a political scandal that embarrassed the Watch. Promotion to his own command was the solution. Known as The Thieftakers, they are the dregs of the Kalider City Watch, destined to spend the rest of their careers hunting criminals in the worst neighbourhoods. After all, what fuss could he cause running down thieves and murderers in the slums?

Old Gate and this murder might be the perfect combination of place and crime to test his theories. The Thieftakers are the best Kalider has at tracking criminals, and Loft must teach them investigative skills to match.

Can he validate his theories and turn the Thieftakers into the first detectives in Kalider?

Analysis:

There's some good stuff hiding in this description, but there were also points where I was a bit bogged down reading it. I want to find myself captivated and drawn along by each sentence.

In copywriting, unlike prose, often it is better to use shorter sentences and try to create a faster rhythm.

I like the idea in the opening hook. I just think it's too long.

Meeks Version:

Loft had just one question…

…why was the murder so violent?

This crime even shocked his veteran Sergeant. Captain Edrin Loft is new to the job. The brutal murder needs solving, but the leads aren't much to go on. And people are watching.

Time is of the essence.

The Thieftakers are the dregs of the Kalider City watch. They hunt the worst of the worst. This is the Captains' new command, and it comes with its own set of challenges. Is he up for the job? Will they follow his lead?

Loft has a few tricks up his sleeve. He believes in science. This may be the perfect case to test out some of his methods, but there's one thing he didn't count on…

If you love Fantasy with a murder mystery to keep you guessing, you'll adore the twists in this tale.

Get it now.

Analysis:

Often I don't like using full names and titles. In many cases, it just isn't necessary. For this description, though, I tried it with and without and felt it sounded better with the full "Captain Edrin Loft." So I mixed up using his last name and title.

Because it's fantasy, I left in the part about the Kalider City watch. Some fantasy names are hard to pronounce when reading. If it's hard to read and the word or name slows me down, I eliminate it. Here, that wasn't the case.

Also, I moved around some of the elements I left it on a bit of a cliffhanger. "But there's one thing he didn't count on..."

I've not read the book. I don't know if there's "one thing" or not, but I'm sure that there must be since it's a mystery. It's a really good hook and leads one naturally to the next line.

CHAPTER FORTY-TWO

DESCRIPTION TWENTY-FOUR - HUMOR AND SATIRE

Author: TL Clark
Title: *Self-Love: A British Tale of Woe and Wit*
Price: $3.99
Genre: Humor and Satire

Before:

What if the most important love...
is the one you have for yourself?

Is it possible for a shrinking violet to grow?
Molly, a bumbling thirty-something single florist with issues, certainly
hopes so.

With her health, happiness, and possibly her sanity hanging in the balance,
Molly must find a way to silence her inner critic, which sounds uncannily
like her mother and just won't shut up.

This is her personal-growth-whilst-shrinking story, sprinkled with toils of
weight loss, dredging dates, flowering friendship and blooming self-
discovery.

As Molly discovers the path to personal growth is no bed of roses, will she blossom or will she wither?

"Fun, quirky, meaningful." ~ Felicia Bates, 5-star Amazon review
"A wonderful and inspiring read." ~ Candi H, 5-star Amazon review
"Well written and funny." ~ Carol Paxman, 5-star Amazon review
"Highly recommend, a very real human story of struggles and successes." ~ djann, 5-star Amazon review

This book is a standalone.
Written by award-winning author, TL Clark.
Suitable for 18+ due to mature content.
Mascara warning; may cause tears of sadness and/or laughter.
May change the way you look at your life.

Analysis:

This one may be too good to improve upon. It's got a nice flow to it, some good laugh lines, and makes one want to know more about the protagonist.

I really like how she wove in the job, florist, with "shrinking violet," "personal growth," and "flowering friendship."

I've written a version that's a little different, but is it better?

"Brian, why would you include a rewrite that wasn't an improvement?"

That's a great question. I want to show how there is value in always trying to improve the copy. It's a good exercise. Some will find it better, some will prefer the original. It will be up to the author to decide if she thinks it's worth testing.

Meeks Version:

Love may be the goal…

…but it will take three things to get there.

Positive self-image, a muzzle for her snarky inner voice, and a willingness to take a chance… or have another glass of wine.

Also, she may have to stop dating guys who are more of a mess than she.

But there is one main question…

Is it possible for a shrinking violet to grow?

Molly, a bumbling, thirty-something, single florist with issues, certainly hopes so.

With her health, happiness, and possibly her sanity hanging in the balance, Molly must find a way to silence her inner critic, which sounds uncannily like her mother, and just won't shut up. "No, I've not considered a pregnancy out of wedlock. And nobody is getting any younger… that's how life works." (This should probably be rewritten by the author in a British accent.)

This is her personal-growth-whilst-shrinking story, sprinkled with toils of weight-loss, dredging dates, flowering friendship, and blooming self-discovery.

As Molly discovers that the path to personal growth is no bed of roses, will she blossom, or will she wither?

You'll come for the snark and stay for the charming story.

Get it now.

Analysis:

> I don't know if my version is better.
> I like it, but only time and data will tell.

CHAPTER FORTY-THREE

Author: Rachel Richards
Title: *The 7-Day Ketogenic Diet Meal Plan - Volume 1*
Price: $4.99
Genre: Health, Fitness & Dieting

Before:

Achieve results with a convenient daily meal plan using these quick and easy recipes. Don't sacrifice taste for a healthy diet.

A ketogenic diet forces your body to burn fat as the primary source of energy.

What is the Ketogenic Diet?

Your body uses what you eat to give you energy. Carbohydrates raise your blood sugar levels, and your body reacts by producing insulin to deal with it. Unfortunately, insulin aids in converting glucose to fat, which is then stored in your body's cells.

A ketogenic diet is designed to make your body burn fat instead of carbohydrates. It is comprised mainly of a high fat diet with low carb foods and normal levels of protein. Carbohydrates are kept below 60g and preferably around the 20g to 40g level on a daily basis. Slight overage once in a while is not too bad, but where possible less than 50g is the best way to go. This keeps the body in a state of ketosis, whereby the body is burning fat as the steady source of energy.

Whilst the actual dietary ingredients of ketosis are important, sensible exercise also plays a big part in losing weight and fine tuning the body's metabolism.

It is essential that you consult your doctor or health professional before embarking on any radical changes in your diet, particularly if you have a lifestyle illness such as diabetes, IBS or any other disease that may be affected by a change in diet.

Most participants of a ketogenic diet plan find that it changes their lives for the better. This high fat, low carb cookbook has create tasty ketogenic diet recipes that make it easy to keep your plan in check. In terms of beverages, drink as much water as possible, but you are also allowed green tea or black coffee. Avoid fizzy drinks, limit alcohol (one drink is fine) and no fruit juices.

The high fat and low carb recipes are designed for up to 4 people. Every person has a different level of carbohydrate tolerance and participates in a different level of daily exercise. To truly work with a ketogenic diet, you must find your level of carbohydrate tolerance. A little trial and error or experimentation may be needed. You may mix and match the meal recipes in this book to your liking. The 7-day meal plan is merely an example.

If you are trying to lose weight, calorie intake is also important. For men, a daily intake of below 2,000 calories is acceptable. For women, the daily intake is around 1,600 calories.

Don't feel like you have to give up on your favorite foods. With recipes like the low carb peanut butter cookies or the chocolate mousse, you can still feed your sweet tooth without feeling guilty.

Inside this book are the following types of meals:

Breakfast - 7 recipes
Lunch - 7 recipes

Snacks - 14 recipes
Dinner - 7 recipes

Ingredient measurements are given in both imperial and metric.

Bonuses Available

A recipe for 'Keto Rolls'; this recipe serves as a great substitute for those missing the taste and feel of bread without adding the carbs.

A free printable version of the meal plan and shopping list is also included.

Download the book now to get started.

Analysis:

In non-fiction, one needs to go a bit longer than fiction because consumers are looking for facts about what's in the book. But one can overdo it. This original description got to be a bit long, and I started to tire while reading it.
This is how I judge length: Does my mind begin to wander?
The information covered was good, but do we need it all?
The opening hook, as you've learned by now, was just too long and not as strong as I felt it could be.

Meeks Version:

Do you hate diets?

Weight-loss can be yummy...

...if you know the secrets of Ketogenic eating.

Don't sacrifice taste for a healthy diet. A ketogenic diet forces your body to burn fat as the primary source of energy.

What is the Ketogenic Diet?

Your body uses what you eat to give you energy. Carbohydrates raise your blood sugar levels, and your body reacts by producing insulin to deal with it.

Why is this bad?

Insulin helps change glucose to fat.

What if your body learned to fuel itself by burning fat?

A ketogenic diet is designed to make your body burn fat instead of carbohydrates. It is comprised mainly of a high-fat diet with low carb foods and normal levels of protein. Carbohydrates are kept below 60g and preferably around the 20g- to 40g-level on a daily basis.

Don't feel like you have to give up your favorite foods. With recipes like the low-carb peanut butter cookies or chocolate mousse, you can still feed your sweet tooth without feeling guilty.

Inside this book are the following types of meals:

Breakfast - 7 recipes
Lunch - 7 recipes
Snacks - 14 recipes
Dinner - 7 recipes

You'll love the results, because watching the weight come off, without hating what you're eating, makes all the difference in the world.

Get it now.

Analysis:

I used the facts from the original and pulled out the most important bits and gave them their own lines to stand out.

The hook is better.

And the length is a bit less, which I think will get the reader to the CTA just as they're ready to buy.

CHAPTER FORTY-FOUR

ARTICLE - THE BURDEN

It's a dark secret.

Indie authors don't like to talk about it...

...but we all know it's true.

The one aspect that doesn't get talked about in the blog posts or news articles but is always present in our minds.

We don't even like to talk about it with each other.

But in hushed tones, maybe off in the corner of a conference, it gets mentioned. And those within whispershot will nod in agreement.

I speak of The Burden.

The Burden that we all share. The Burden some have trouble handling.

The Burden that is the life of an Indie Author.

We are SO FREAKING AWESOME.

It can be too much at times.

Awesomeness isn't to be taken lightly.

There are people who work in offices and cubicles that will never know the joy of getting a 5-star review from someone who didn't give birth to you.

They will never know the joy of royalty revenue.

Their lives will NOT be spent creating worlds, friends, and lovers doing the most amazing things.

They'll never know the happiness that comes with naming a character after someone who pissed you off in high school—and then killing them.

We travel to the stars with, solve the greatest mysteries of, and dig into the souls of the most interesting people in the universe... our people... the ones we lovingly built.

That's pretty FREAKING AWESOME.

Is it hard?

Yes, but in the best possible way.

Do civilians understand?

Yes, and they're jealous. Being AWESOME is a burden.

I know that every one of you has felt this burden… because YOU ARE AWESOME, TOO.

Don't let your own AWESOMENESS weigh you down. Just accept it.

And keep writing books.

This has been a public service announcement.

Now back to your regularly scheduled group posts.

CHAPTER FORTY-FIVE

DESCRIPTION TWENTY-SIX - ORGANIZED CRIME AND SUSPENSE

Author: O.N. Stefan
Title: *Deeds of Darkness: An Amanda Blake thriller with a massive twist (Book 2)*
Price: $0.99
Genre: Organized Crime and Suspense

Before:

Discover a crime thriller which will have you in its grip from the explosive start to one of the most shocking endings of the year.

Leave the past where it belongs, Amanda Blake is warned by her family, but she can't - an old love letter and faded snapshot are leading her down a very deadly path.

As her investigation leads her deeper into an underbelly of illegal activities, everyone she loves will be put into the line of fire.

Amanda has to decide who she can trust, and who is out to destroy her.

The stakes are high and there's no turning back even at the cost of her own life.

This sequel to the Deadly Caress leads the reader on a classic chase of murder and mystery. It will leave you guessing until the last page. Mel Deacon, reviewer.

Read this spell-binding thriller today.

Analysis:

At this point, I've talked plenty about the need for the blank lines to make the description less of a block of text, so I won't say it again...

Okay, maybe I will. Giant blocks of text are worse than being thrown in a Russian Gulag for 27 years.

Don't do it.

There are some good parts. We just need to let them shine a little more by giving them space.

And the opening line is an abomination. It's not a hook. It's too long. It made me want to dig out my eyes with a spoon... that had been recently used to measure out lime juice.

One more thing... why is a Book 2 priced at 99 cents?

Meeks Version:

She was warned.

Don't dig up the past.

The faded love letter, though, wouldn't let her leave it alone.

As Amanda looks at the snapshot, holds the letter, and remembers, something inside of her changes. She can't live without answers, but will those answers get her killed?

In the seedy underbelly of crime and tears, she starts her journey. Who can she trust? Who is out to destroy her?

The stakes are high, and there's no turning back.

You'll love this thriller, because the twists and turns will keep you guessing.

Get it now.

Analysis:

I used the meat of her original version to craft a tighter description with better hooks.

This is the thing about descriptions, as most people have written them.

The synopsis they created usually has the elements of a properly written description, and all one needs to do is shift things about and turn facts into questions. Those make better hooks and keep the reader moving along.

She wasn't far off.

Now it will convert more of the lookie-loos into reader-loos.

CHAPTER FORTY-SIX

Author: T.J. Quinn
Title: *Ice Princess – A Sci-Fi Alien Romance*
Price: $2.99
Genre: Alien Romance Science Fiction

Before:

Zorban was first in line to become king of Thalia, once he finds his soul mate and marries her. The very night he finds her, she vanishes.

Devastated at the loss of his soulmate, he goes to Earth to make a new life for himself.

When he meets Leah, at his best friend's wedding celebration, his whole body reacted to her.

He never expected to feel that way about anyone but his soulmate.

How could he feel this way about a human from another world?

Analysis:

Sadly, the opening hook made me stop reading. I didn't believe the premise, because finding a soul mate could take years or decades. I just didn't believe that's how a king would be crowned.

That doesn't mean it isn't believable in the story, but when we find out that piece of information, there may be a better explanation.

The next thing that bothered me was that in the next line, "soulmate" was spelled as one word, whereas it was just spelled as two words in line one. Not only is it echoing (using the same distinctive word in close proximity to where it was used before), but it's also not consistent.

Line three is just a little bit generic.

And though it finishes with an attempt at a hook and not a call-to-action, it's not a strong hook.

Meeks Version:

About to ascend to the throne…

…Prince Zoban loses everything.

Where has his soul mate gone?

In their world, Thalia, soul mates are real. From birth, they search for each other, and when they connect, the depth of their understanding of how it should be, removes any doubt. When "the one" for Prince Zoban disappears, chaos reigns in the kingdom. Is it his uncle who took her?

The prince can't become King without his mate.

The royal line is threatened.

Zoban must go to Earth. It's the only way to save him, but when he gets to this strange world, his life takes another turn. The prince is sure he will be alone forever.

Does destiny have other plans?

Can a miracle happen?

You'll adore this science fiction alien romance because of the intrigue and twists. It will keep you turning the pages.

Get it now.

Analysis:

The thing about romance books is that there are certain tropes that are expected by the readers. I tried to hint that the reader will find these ideas that they love without giving away too much.

The word "destiny" has a bit of hook to it by its very nature. We all want to find out the "how" that destiny plays out in the story.

And then there's the idea of a plot to steal the throne. That's another piece that should draw the readers into the tale.

Of course, and I've said this on almost every other description, the formatting is such that it's light and easy to read, which makes it more likely the potential new fan will get from line one to "get it now."

It should be noted that I chose to start working on this description at 5:00 am and the author wasn't available for questions. So I read the "Look inside," which helped.

But the real key for me was reading the book's 5-star reviews. They gave me a better understanding of how the folks who had already enjoyed the book felt.

If you're writing a description before the book is released, obviously this isn't an option. You may have feedback from your ARC team, though, so don't just think of their notes as being for edits. Use the positive to help with your copywriting.

CHAPTER FORTY-SEVEN

Author: T.J. Quinn
Title: *Vrak's Bride: Mail Order Brides Alien Mate Romance (Galactic Brides Book 2)*
Price: $2.99
Genre: Alien Romance

Before:

The last thing Vrak had in mind was getting a wife to share the lonely life he had chosen for himself in Sumirion. But the minute he laid eyes on that human female, he knew his life had changed forever. But Aliyah wasn't meant for him. She was contracted to be another man's wife and his job was to deliver her to him.

Living on a devastated Earth, Aliyah is ready to leave. Her only way out is to join a Mail Order Bride Agency and marry an alien she has never seen. With almost no food and no medicines left, she doesn't have much choice and after giving it some thought, she finally joined the agency. A few weeks later she traveled to a planet called Sumirion to marry a warrior. By the time she arrived, she had second thoughts about the whole thing, though she had no other choice. Meeting Vrak only made things even harder for her. A terrible storm bought them a bit of time but it wasn't enough. Vrak would face big trouble to get what he wants – his woman.

Analysis:

The opening is much too long. And it isn't compelling. From there on, it's just a little too much synopsis and not enough hint. The whole "love at first sight" trope may be great for romance novels, but I don't think it plays as well on a description.

Do I need to mention the giant blocks of text?

Meeks Version:

Earth's days are numbered…

…the only way to survive is to leave.

And for women, this means joining an agency.

Throughout the galaxy, aliens seek brides. On Earth, after the devastation brought by the wars, food and medicine are in scarce supply. There doesn't seem to be any hope. If Aliyah wants to survive, she's got one choice… become a mail order bride for alien suitors.

Then it happened.

On a planet called Sumirion, a warrior wants to marry Aliyah. She's not thrilled and is starting to wonder if it was the right choice, but it's too late. An alien named Vrak arrives to deliver Aliyah to her new husband.

Then the storm hit.

Will their time together lead to romance?

Will Vrak risk everything to break her contract on Sumirion?

You'll adore this tale of interspecies romance, because love is the same throughout the universe.

Get it now.

Analysis:

This is pretty straightforward. I set the scene, explained the important point about Earth's issues, and then hinted at the romance and the potential consequences for Vrak.

CHAPTER FORTY-EIGHT

DESCRIPTION TWENTY - HISTORICAL ROMANCE

Author: Kimberly Kennedy
Title: *The Last Chance*
Price: $0.99
Genre: Historical Romance

Before:

NOT SUITABLE FOR ANYONE UNDER 18

Chance Riley's life as a mob enforcer in 1920's Chicago, has left him cold and hard. He feels nothing anymore, except when he's near her.

The one woman he can't have.

The beautiful Emma feels trapped in her life as an arm decoration to the head gangster and secretly yearns for his right hand man.

What would happen if these two finally take a chance at feeling more than frozen in the life they've chosen. Will they burn up in each other's arms or find themselves dead at the hands of a betrayed boss.

The Last Chance is the first SHORT EROTICA in the Historical Hots series brought to you by Kimberly Kennedy. Please note that this book is a very hot sensual short for adult only so if you are easily offend by sexy situations then please do not read.

Analysis:

There are bits in here that are good.

Mostly, though, it's a disaster with a side of "no."

First, do we need the last name for Chance? No, we do not. In copywriting, we want tight copy, so extraneous words have to go.

There is one more personal preference I have, which is NOT a rule or law or edict or even a suggestion, but you should follow it anyway because it would make me happy.

Rule #1: Don't use the word "Feel."

I should have mentioned that I have used this word in my writing, back in the early days, and might have even overused it.

But an author I respect said it was lazy writing. There are lots of ways to convey feeling something without just saying, "She felt something."

Will your children start to get bullied at school because one of their parents used "feel" in one of their novels?

Yes, they will. It will be brutal. They'll be scarred for life, and you'll start drinking to excess because of the guilt. (Note: I could have said you'd feel bad, but that's what you were expecting from me.)

I digress.

I do like the bit about the 1920s, as it paints a good visual.

Now, as for, "…if these two take a chance at feeling more frozen than the life they've chosen…"

> I do not like description rhymes.
> I do not like them all the time.
> I do not like them in chick lit.
> I do not like them in spec fic.
> I do not like them in Sci-Fi.
> I do not like them with a plate of fries.

…I could go on, but I think you sort of get where I'm going with this homage to Theodore Geisel.

And lastly, I understand the need to sometimes include disclaimers. It makes sense in erotica. I do not understand the wanton disregard for our friend the comma.

In short, this could be better.

Meeks Version:

When rules got broken…

…the boss calls Chance.

What if Chance broke rule #1?

When Emma met the mob boss, it was all glamour, but that didn't last. Her life became a string of parties and loneliness, because she was little more than arm candy.

Could she find more?

Chance's life was about a routine he hated, but he couldn't get out of it if he wanted. Each day was like the one before: find the thug and make him pay —because you can't let a guy break the rules.

Rule number one… nobody touches Emma.

But what if he did?

What if he can't help it?

Sometimes love at first sight can get you dead.

You'll love this Historical Romance because of the steam, but you'll tell your friends because of the story.

Get it now.

Analysis:

I really liked my "You'll…because" in this one. I don't know if people will tell their friends more than they would otherwise, but why not put the seed in their minds?

CHAPTER FORTY-NINE

ARTICLE - YOUR FIRST INSTINCT

Your first instinct is usually right…

…except when it's horribly wrong.

Authors face decisions every day. Should I write or market? Is my description as good as it could be?

Should I kill off that character I named after the bully who used to pick on me in sixth grade and despite his having died a horrible death in his twenties still pisses me off?

I often learn things about myself while playing chess.

Today, it was a game against a player whose rating was 80 points higher than mine. He should win most of the time.

The opening, for those of you who are chess nerds, was the Queen's Gambit Declined: Chigorin Defense.

I was playing black.

Early on, I exchanged a bishop for his knight and traded queens.

Since he was a better player, I figured simplifying the position would give me a better chance.

On the 16th move, I saw what I THOUGHT was a surefire way to win an exchange.

I took his pawn with my knight, he captured back with his pawn, and I recaptured that pawn with my rook.

"But Brian, that sounds like you lost the exchange? Two pawns for a knight is a bad deal."

Yes, it is, but his bishop and knight were lined up and attacked by my rook, so I would get one of them…

…or so I thought.

My joy turned to sorrow when I saw he could defend the bishop, which meant the knight behind it was safe too.

My FIRST instinct was that I had made a blunder.

IT WAS WRONG.

Keep in mind, this is blitz chess—we were playing 5-minute games, and I had to move quickly. Instinct is a part of the game because I couldn't do deep analysis with so little time.

But using a little time to check my assumption, which was that I had made a blunder and his defense had spoiled my plan, I realized it had been a good idea.

For five seconds, I pouted.

Then I looked at the board and asked, "Am I sure it was a blunder?"

I was NOT sure.

You see, while it was true that he'd defended the bishop once, he could NOT add any more defense to that piece.

AND…

I could bring in another rook to add to the attack.

Which I did…

…and he had no choice but to trade his bishop for one pawn. That left me up one pawn in the exchange.

On move 30, I won by checkmate.

Now how does this apply to authors?

Many are often quick to self-criticize.

The first instinct upon any sort of adversity (perceived or real) is to assume the worst.

Have you ever done that?

Well, here's the good news, you have time on the clock. The moment your stomach ties itself in knots because you're sure you've messed up, take five seconds and pout…

…then look at the board and ask, "Am I sure this was a blunder?"

Once you let your brain relax, you may see other possibilities or solutions.

In one of my novels, it seemed like I had written myself into only one possible ending. And it was rather blah. I just didn't think it was good enough.

But what could I do?

I stopped writing.

There were other projects, so I shifted gears and let my mind ponder the state of the story for a bit.

Then I kept pondering.

I pondered so much that a layer of ponder scum built up over time.

Nine months after I had stopped just short of finishing the novel, an idea popped into my head as I was walking down the boardwalk in Atlantic City.

Four days later, the book was done.

Checkmate!

CHAPTER FIFTY

Author: Rebecca Moesta and Kevin J. Anderson
Title: *Crystal Doors 1 Island Realm*
Price: $3.99
Genre: Steampunk

Before:

Fourteen-year-old cousins Gwen and Vic have lived together ever since the mysterious deaths of Gwen's parents and disappearance of Vic's mother - until Vic's scientist father accidentally transports them through a magical doorway to the island of Elantra, a wonder-filled place of magic as well as steampunk technology. Vic and Gwen are soon caught in a tempest of ancient magic, bizarre gadgets, vicious creatures, and fierce battles - in a territorial feud with the sea-dwelling merlons, an age-old conflict between the bright and dark sages... and Gwen and Vic's own mysterious roots.

Analysis:

I'm not going to go all snarky, as I'm wont to do, on an author who has written many books in the Dune and Star Wars worlds. And there is some good in there.

We all know about the giant block of text. That's not helpful.

So, what else?

Well, all of the ingredients for hooks and intrigue are built into this description, and admittedly, for an author of his stature, the true fans may not need to be hooked as hard as someone who isn't familiar with his work.

The descriptions, though, will reach both kinds of potential readers. We want them all to buy the books.

Meeks Version:

The doorway was magical.

The teleportation was an accident.

Can Vic and Gwen survive?

On a magical island with bizarre gadgets, ancient magic, and vicious creatures, a battle is brewing. For Vic and Gwen, it is an extraordinary adventure, but the danger is real.

Three factions struggle for control. Sea-dwelling merlons, bright mages, and dark mages, all want to rule, but in this age-old struggle, who will win?

Who should Vic and Gwen trust?

And there's a secret about Vic that he doesn't know.

Will the truth about his mysterious roots in this world undo everything?

You'll enjoy this adventure, because it blends Atlantis with steampunk and magic.

Get it now.

Analysis:

In the post-writing analysis, Kevin J Anderson agreed that this was a better version of the description.

Then the real test—we showed it to his wife. She agreed, too.

The point is, he's sold books in some of the greatest franchises of all time, Dune and Star Wars, yet even an author with 80 titles to his name can still learn something new.

Today, in Bali, it was description-writing.

CHAPTER FIFTY-ONE

DESCRIPTION THIRTY-ONE - MYTHS & LEGENDS

Author: J.T. Williams
Title: *Half-Bloods Rising*
Price: $0.99
Genre: Myths & Legends

Before:

Book one temporarily discounted to celebrate the release of the climactic finale of the series, The Last Dwemhar, available now!

Epic fantasy readers praise Half-Bloods Rising:

"Fast-paced and held me on edge! I couldn't put it down!" – 5-Star Amazon review

"Good lore and magic development cannot wait to learn more in future books. I would recommend this to anyone interested in a solid fantasy book!" – 5-star Amazon review

"...I was hooked. The main character development was spot on. I especially enjoyed the ending of the book which was an explosive unexpected turn of events. Looking forward to book 2!" – 5-star Amazon review

"A totally different look at the elven people and a pretty dark book.......CAN NOT WAIT to read the next one!" – 5-star Amazon review

"I love to lose myself in a good story in a different world than the one I live in. This book delivered that and more. I recommend this book especially if you are a fan of fantasy." – 5-star Amazon review

The elves have been called to war. As his parents leave, Kealin and his siblings stay behind to continue to train for the inevitable bloodshed that will reach their shores. For all of his life, he has been persecuted for being half-elf but his mother's true lineage was a guarded secret. She has been in hiding and he will soon discover why.

A prophecy is revealed that foretells doom for all the warriors who departed. In order to avert the disaster, Kealin and his half-blood siblings embark into the frigid seas of the north aboard an enchanted ship. In a perilous journey, Kealin discovers a power that is not elven in nature. He is changing. As the blood of an ancient race surges in his veins, a power awakens within his mind tying him to a powerful and dangerous culture.

But what else is waking in the long-frozen north, will risk all of them and Kealin is playing into the hands of a master deceiver. He must learn to control this new power before a hidden plot destroys everyone he seeks to save.

Analysis:

I've changed my position.

Quotes at the beginning do work, but they are also against Amazon's T.O.S. And while I've had quotes for years in many of my descriptions and never had problems, I no longer think it's a good idea.

Violating Amazon's T.O.S. is never a good idea, but that's not the main reason I've decided against them.

I don't believe they're as strong as the short opening hooks you can write.

They simply add too much weight and too many words to the description.

The two main negatives here are too much synopsis and a bit of echoing with the word "power." It's used a bunch of times.

Meeks Version:

With his father gone to war…

…and his mother in hiding…

…Kealin must make a decision.

Should they stay and train to defend their elven land, like their father asked, or head out into the icy waters to try to change fate?

When he realizes how much danger their parents are in, Kealin and his siblings take to the seas in a magical vessel. The voyage doesn't go as planned. They know the prophecy. Can it really be true?

Something has happened. There is a power on board, but it isn't elven in nature. What does it all mean, and how will it change Kealin?

Not all who appear to help are friends.

Who can they trust?

You'll adore this gripping story of sword and sorcery, because the characters keep you hooked until the end.

Get it now.

Analysis:

What do you think improved?

CHAPTER FIFTY-TWO

DESCRIPTION THIRTY-TWO: WITCHES & WIZARDS

Author: Mona Marple
Title: *A Devil of a Time (A Witch in Time Book 2)*
Price: $2.99
Genre: Witches & Wizards

Before:

"Would you travel in the past to right a wrong?
   Solve a cold case?
   Catch a killer?
   Meet the 5 witches who will."

Felicity Octavia Geraldine Warner the Fourth - Flick when her family aren't around - is desperately attempting to hide from her strong witch lineage and live a normal life, until her Gram cuts off her access to the family wealth unless she agrees to marry a powerful wizard.

Needing an income of her own, Flick applies for every job she sees. Including one with the Agency of Paranormal Peculiarities.

Before she knows it, she's hired - and sent back in time to 1999 to solve a cold case. A dead body has been discovered in the Old Bailey and it's down to Flick to solve the case, using magic she has avoided her whole life.

It's time for Flick to accept who she is and discover the truth with the help of a Black Dog ghost, and in just seven days.

This title is part of the A Witch in Time Mystery series. Each book stands completely on its own, but you'll have more fun if you read them all together!

Analysis:

I frequently advise authors to avoid using both first and last name because it isn't important. I've never needed to advise an author to eliminate the second, third, fourth, and the number.

We can either use Felicity or Flick, because when the potential reader gets into the story, they'll get all of the other names.

There is value in prose to create such fanciful names. But it doesn't help copywriting.

There are elements in here that could be hooks if they were just massaged a bit.

Let's give it a try.

Meeks Version:

Felicity must choose…

…live a normal life and be cut off…

…or embrace her powers.

Her decision gets harder when her grandmother arranges for her to marry a powerful wizard. If she's going to avoid that disaster, she'll need to find a job… and that's where everything changes.

The Agency of Paranormal Peculiarities needs investigators. Felicity is perfect for the job, but there's just one catch: she'll need to use the powers she's been trying to avoid. Is giving up her dream of a normal life worth it?

Can she learn to embrace who she is?

Will the decision get her in over her head?

Sent back in time to 1999, Felicity must solve a murder at the Old Bailey.

This one will be a challenge, and there's a catch: she's got just seven days to solve it.

You'll love this story because of the struggle and the twists.

Get it now.

Analysis:

Here, I took the important themes and focused on them, and like in the analysis of the original, I stripped out the unnecessary bits.

Also, I took out the disclaimer. I don't believe that helps the cause.

CHAPTER FIFTY-THREE

DESCRIPTION THIRTY-THREE: GODDESSES AND ANGELS

Author: JL Madore
Title: *Watcher Untethered: Dark Angels Paranormal Romance (Watcher of the Gray Book 1)*
Price: $0.99
Genre: Goddess and Angels

Before:

Duty. Honor. My brothers. That's all I have.

Wounded in battle, Zander wakes in a daemon feeding ground, bound to a human female. The origins of the restraints are unknowns, the woman - Austin - a task for Otherworld exposure. In the midst of human corpses, and with the relationship punishable by death, Austin tempts a part of him he's locked down his entire existence. His beast, however, the part of him that consumes every dark soul he's ever dispatched, pull at its tether, fighting to claim what can never be.

The watchers of the Gray Series by JL Madore, joins the gritty, dark paranormal romance traditions of JR Ward, Sherrilyn Kenyon, and IT Lucas.

Devour this page-turner and join the secret world of the Watchers of the Gray!

Analysis:

The first line is pretty good. It's hookish, though I do think it could be better.

This description's problem is that I didn't know what was going on. I was lost at the part about the restraints, then I got lost again about the tethering.

Also, the CTA was too long.

Meeks Version:

He had finally learned control.

Now it was all at risk.

Facing death can change a man's will.

In a dungeon, bound to a human female, Zander has to make a decision. Should he unleash the beast within? This means giving up the years of suppressing it and abandoning his dreams of normalcy.

The beast within him consumes dark souls. If he's not careful, it might claim him, too.

But that isn't the biggest threat—falling in love is forbidden and punishable by death.

Can he save the woman, himself, and love… and survive?

The odds are against it.

You'll love the thrill ride of this goddess and angels story, because it will keep you turning pages.

Get it now.

Analysis:

This daemon novel seems to have a lot of elements in it based upon the description she started with, but I'm not entirely sure, as I've not read it.

In most cases, I wrote these descriptions while either on Skype with the author or got on and discussed it afterward.

This one, however, was written while the author flew home from 20BooksBali, and I worked on it without her feedback. I mentioned this because it was a challenge.

One thing that did help is that I had a friend in Bali who read what I wrote, has experience in similar genres, and pointed out a HUGE blunder I made.

Where I wrote, "Can he save the woman, himself, and love...", I had "girl" for woman, which comes from my 50's noir mystery voice. In that era, "girl" was more commonly used, but the readership for this book, which is likely women, would have been offended.

I didn't even notice. (I was clubbing a mastodon in a really manly way as I wrote it and made the blunder.)

No matter how much you think you know something, it's always a good idea to get feedback from other eyes, because a single word can make all the difference.

CHAPTER FIFTY-FOUR

DESCRIPTION THIRTY-FOUR: PARANORMAL ROMANCE

Author: Lena Fox
Title: *Strawberry (Vampire Temptations 1)*
Price: Permafree (series price point 3.99)
Genre: Paranormal Romance

Before:

Held captive by a vampire in love with her blood…

Out of work actress Kitty French knows her new role as a vampire's sexy victim is dodgy, but she needs the cash.

She never thought it would leave her at the mercy of a real vampire…

A vampire who thinks she's the tastiest of them all.

She'll do anything to escape his cold lips alive, because being part of a blood-sucker's ongoing meal plan isn't high on her list of life goals, no matter how sexy he is. How can she make him see she's more than just food?

Learning vampires are real is one thing. What happens after that she would never see coming…

186 · BRIAN D. MEEKS

Strawberry is the first book in the adults-only Vampire Temptations series by Lena Fox.

If you love brooding vampire men, steamy sex scenes, light horror, sassy, food-obsessed heroines, and a H.E.A with a twist, click Buy Now and sink your teeth into this fresh and fun novel today.

Analysis:

This isn't bad, but I do think the good hook elements are a bit buried in the copy.

Meeks Version:

It was just a role…

…or so she thought.

"Vampire's sexy victim" sounded fun—until she learned it was real.

Actress Kitty French needs the money. As they say, "There aren't any small roles…" but this gig is not what it seems. The first clue was his cold lips. And then there was the bite.

It was clear from the look on his chiseled face, he liked the taste of her.

Can Kitty show him she's more than just a snack?

She's playing a dangerous game, but she's in too deep to stop.

You'll love the brooding vampires, steamy sex scenes, sassy, food-obsessed heroines, and a H.E.A with a twist, because this book is fresh and fun.

Get it now.

Analysis:

This one is short and to the point. I did like her last paragraph, so I took most of it and then added the CTA to the end.

CHAPTER FIFTY-FIVE

ARTICLE - QUESTIONS YOU NEED TO ASK
She was terrified…
…the fear crippled her, and the pain was tremendous.
Nobody told her that being an Indie author was like being in school.
And she realized she hadn't studied for the final.
Final Exam Questions:
1) Do you know the read-through from book 1 to 2 in your series?
2) Did you break it out by Sales and KU Downloads?
3) If you raised your book price from 99 cents to $4.99, what will happen to the number of KU downloads you'll get?
4) Do you know how to analyze a price change?
5) How long should you leave a new price up before you have enough data to draw conclusions?
6) Is it more important to analyze the impact on page reads or sales?
7) Should you just do what all the successful authors are doing, knowing they've probably never tested other prices and were just doing what everyone else did before, because you know that following untested ideas is a GREAT marketing strategy and it WON'T probably cost you tens of thousands of dollars in missed opportunities?
8) Do you know your KENPC numbers for your books?
9) Do you calculate ROI?
10) Do you study the daily variance of your sales and page reads to understand how much they can change without ANY change in price?
These are the questions for the Beginner Indie Author 101 final.
Are you ready?

―――――

Okay… there isn't a final.

But there's a dearth of information about WHAT WE need to know out there.

Math-phobes will be shaking violently. Some will be curled up in the fetal position. Others will be adding me to a list of people they wish to one day punish.

It's not as bad as it sounds.

All of those questions require fairly basic math.

Math that even people who "can't do math" can do.

So don't be afraid to broaden your horizons.

Think about the questions.

See if you can answer them. If you do that, it may be a bit of a struggle, but in a short amount of time, you'll realize it's MUCH easier than you thought.

And it will help you make more money.

Have a great day, folks.

CHAPTER FIFTY-SIX

Description Thirty-Five: YA Fantasy Paranormal Romance

Author: Catherine Banks
Title: *Song of the Moon (Book 1)*
Price: $0.99
Genre: Young Adult Fantasy Paranormal Romance

Before:

What if you found out that there was another world inside your own? What if all of the things you thought made you weird, actually made you powerful? Artemis's life is changed forever when the mysterious man from her dreams, Ares, comes to claim her as his mate. The seventeen year old girl must find a way to adapt to her true life and accept her fate or run from it. She must overcome her fears and human ideals to give her self to the dangerous world, and man, that is her destiny.

Analysis:

The only places where a giant block is acceptable is if you're friends with Jennifer Lopez, a left-tackle, or as a finely aged Gouda. In descriptions, it is verboten.

I give her marks for trying to start with a hook.

But here's the problem with, "What if you found out there was another world inside your own?"

When I see that question, I'm not on the edge of my chair waiting to find out what the next bit of copy might be. Instead, I'm leaning back in my desk chair, scratching my beard, and mentally answering the question in the snarkiest possible way.

1. I'd check the real estate listings there. Since the view has to be crap, there must be bargains.
2. I'd probably go to Snopes and see what they had to say about it.
3. I might consider taking a selfie there and then devote seven to ten hours attempting to craft the perfect hashtag.

By this point, I've gone so far off into the "other world inside my head" that I've lost the desire to even buy a new book.

Still, I do like questions—just not this one.

And not speaking directly to the reader. As you know by now, if you've read this far, I love "bringing the reader in" with "You'll love…because." I'm talking directly to them, but not until I've set the hook.

And then there's the second question: "What if all the things you thought made you weird, actually made you powerful?"

I'm a little offended that the description assumes I have self-confidence issues.

I don't.

Let's try to do better.

Meeks Version:

Is the world moving too quickly?

Artemis thinks so.

But she has no idea what's coming

At seventeen, Artemis has a lot going on in her life. Her mind races all the time. It seems that just making it through the day is a puzzle to be solved. It's exhausting. And her sleep has been crap. The dreams won't stop.

Then she sees him.

A man, whom she's never met, that looks exactly like the fellow in her dreams.

Why is he there?

In a world she never knew existed, Artemis must change how she thinks. Self-doubt can get you killed. And for all the danger, a chance at love is worth the risk.

You'll love this fast-paced story, because everyone enjoys a sexy werewolf and a quest for love.

Get it now.

Analysis:

I focused on the struggles she was having as a seventeen-year-old girl. The description hints at the importance of being self-confident, which lets the reader know there will be growth in the character. And, of course, we need to mention the possibility of romance.

The fact that this book is about werewolf romance wasn't mentioned until I "brought the reader" into the description in the last line before the CTA.

The cover makes it clear that this is a werewolf story, so I didn't feel a need to mention that in the main part of the description.

CHAPTER FIFTY-SEVEN

DESCRIPTION THIRTY-SIX: YA FANTASY PARANORMAL ROMANCE

Author: Catherine Banks
Title: *Kiss of a Star (Book 2)*
Price: $2.99
Genre: Young Adult Fantasy Paranormal Romance

Before:

Artemis' life completely changed when she met Ares and learned of her true genetics. Achilles comes to her and her life is changed yet again as she learns more about herself and Ares' past. Now nothing is simple and life is anything but calm. As she adjusts to her new life she learns that shedding a little blood is more than necessary and that she must do whatever she can to stay with her pack and her mate. Can she figure out a way to protect her pack and stand against the man hunting her? Or will treachery and deceit separate her from the first family she's ever had?

Analysis:

This is the second book in the series. I did the first three for Catherine, and then she and I did the fourth one together.

My analysis from the last one still stands: giant blocks of text are bad.

It's not much of a first line, and this is mostly just a synopsis.

Meeks Version:

Which holds more power?

Truth or love?

Would her secret destroy her mind?

Artemis's life turned upside down the moment she met Ares. He told her things she couldn't believe. Life was a blur—could it all be true? What would that mean?

Before anything, Artemis must get her bearings if she wants to stay with her mate. Each day Artemis is changing, how can she protect her pack?

Enter Achilles, and with him, more questions.

Treachery and deceit are all around.

The stakes grow as this tale unfolds. As more of the world is explored and understood, it becomes clear that nothing will be the same. Can Artemis learn to wield her powers in time?

You'll love this fast-paced adventure, because everyone loves a struggle between good and evil and love and honor.

Get it now.

Analysis:

I spent a lot of time reading through reviews to find the points people seemed to most enjoy about these books. Reviews, for folks who are replacing existing descriptions are a gold mine of potential hooks and hints.

Also, I pulled the parts I liked best from the original.

This version was not exactly as I first wrote it. When I reread my first version, I sensed I'd gone too far with avoiding spoilers, so I went back and reread the original.

There were some powerful words in there that I had glossed over. Most notably, "pack" and "mate." I also found I had used the word "change" or variants thereof, too often.

Always be on the lookout for echoing. The overuse of one word is just lazy if there are other words that will do.

The important point here is, don't be afraid to read and re-read what you've written for your new description. Ask for help in FB groups, and see what those folks say.

Of course, don't just take every opinion as solid gold. Most people still write descriptions as a synopsis of the book, and you don't want to be fooled into going back to bad habits.

CHAPTER FIFTY-EIGHT

Description Thirty-Seven: YA Fantasy Paranormal Romance

Author: Catherine Banks
Title: *Healed by Fire (Book 3)*
Price: $2.99
Genre: Young Adult Fantasy Paranormal Romance

Before:

"The dark approaches. Fire will consume and restore, happiness and pain must be experienced collectively. Death for three will be the end."

Her memory taken and her whereabouts unknown Artemis is taken in by a coven of witches who give her the name Chandra. After an intense interaction with the Beta of the Werewolves, whom she can't deny a connection to, Chandra learns that there are people who know her true identity and that she's not the only halfbreed werewolf alive. Is he really her mate? Just who was she in this previous life? Does she even want to find out the truth? And can she decipher the meaning of her death prophecy before it's too late?

Analysis:

This is a little different than the first two in that she starts with a quote. It's unattributed, though, which made me stop reading to try to figure out if it was from a reader or from the book. Then she falls into the all-too-common synopsis.

I was put off by the use of "taken" twice in the first ten words. She could have used "Her memory erased" instead of "Her memory taken." I truly believe that if one does such a thing in their description, it will hurt conversions. Some readers may fear that the whole novel has such lazy writing.

Of course, it happens to most of us. I'm constantly finding I've echoed words and do my best to choose alternatives. So I don't want to be too hard on her in this instance.

Echoing is an easy thing to do, and it's hard to spot when it's your own writing. Often I only catch it when I'm rereading something aloud.

The point, though, is it's not a good thing, so try to keep duplicate words out of your description.

I do think there are elements in here we can work with. Let's see how I do.

Meeks Version:

Her memory is gone.

She's in a strange place. A century has passed.

Who can she trust?

They've taken her in, but they call her Chandra. Why don't they know her name is Artemis?

Artemis wants to trust the witches and Draco Blu. Does she have any choice?

She's connected with the beta of the werewolves and is learning that her secret has gotten out. Are there other halfbreeds? She may not be the only one.

As she struggles to remember, she can't shake the feeling that he may be her real mate. But that's not her biggest problem. The death prophecy has her worried.

Can she decipher it in time to change fate?

You'll love this third installment in the series, because the action gets taken up a notch.

Get it now.

Analysis:

The thing I want to point out about the second line, is the second sentence, "A century has passed."

I added that later. In the reviews for the book, I noticed some mildly negative comments about the time lapse from book 2 to 3, so this was a great opportunity to address that issue for the reader.

Why not try to prevent the loss of a star or two on future reviews?

CHAPTER FIFTY-NINE

DESCRIPTION THIRTY-EIGHT: YA FANTASY PARANORMAL ROMANCE

Author: Catherine Banks
Title: *Taming Darkness (Book 4)*
Price: $3.99
Genre: Young Adult Fantasy Paranormal Romance

Before:

Things aren't going like anyone planned and life keeps throwing one curve ball after another at Artemis and Ares. Can she live up to the prophecy or have they been wrong this entire time? Join them as they try to right the balance of light and dark in the final installment of the Artemis Lupine Series.

Analysis:

She gets points for the price on this fourth book being $3.99 instead of $2.99. The description, though, is weak.

In this synopsis, I simply get confused. "Can she live up to the prophecy or have they been wrong the entire time?" It just left me not wanting to read on further.

Now, admittedly, the fourth book in a series doesn't need as strong a description as the others unless the author plans to sell a lot of them out of order. This works with some series, where each book is truly its own story and can stand alone.

If that's the case, then all the descriptions are equally important.

Meeks and Catherine Version:

What will Ares find...

...in death's realm?

The final battle is imminent.

Caught in limbo, he faces off with Death in a battle of wits. If he wins, Ares gets back their souls. If he loses, Death has other plans for them. Can Ares wield his words as well as he does his sword?

Maurice is king, but the resistance and his traitorous son are still free. He must put them down if his place on the throne is to be secure. Killing is easy, but there are challenges.

Will he be able to outmaneuver Ares and Victor?

This battle needs the werewolves, dragons, and sidhe joining together. Darkness and light will fight for world domination. The can be only one winner.

You'll love this final installment, because you won't see the ending coming.

Get it now.

Analysis:

As I mentioned earlier, we did this last one together.

Writing descriptions is hard. It's especially challenging to write one for your own book, because you know what happens and want to share all the yummy details.

Catherine has made great progress with her copywriting, but there were still a few instances where a word was changed to make it less "on the mark" and more "hint at what might be."

The other interesting change we made was in the first longer paragraph.

The first sentence ended with "wills," and we later decided that "wits" was more interesting and a better hook.

This led to the third sentence of that paragraph which, when compared to the original, was much stronger and had a length more pleasing to the eye.

Remember: we always want there to be a few parts to the description that have some meat on them. It can't be all short lines.

CHAPTER SIXTY

ARTICLE - BARNES AND NOBLE ADVERTISING ANALYSIS

This is a post I wrote for both my Mastering Amazon Ads: An Author's Guide and the 20BooksTo50K groups. It's another example of pretty solid copywriting.

Dear Wide Authors,

Barnes & Noble announces ads…

…but is it a good thing?

I know you may not like math, but if you're Wide and have been thinking you'd love to have an AMS like option on the other platforms, then you may be thrilled.

"Not so fast my friend," he said, channeling his inner Lee Corso.

The range of CPM (Cost Per Mille or Cost per 1,000) is $12.00 on the low end, to $7.00 if you buy 1 million impressions. (That's a $7,000 commitment.)

Can you make money?

Maybe, but let's look at what will happen for most people.

Hint: It will be a trail of tears.

Those are spectacularly high costs per mille.

It seems that Barnes & Noble is focused more on their bottom line than building a platform that can be profitable for authors.

Of course, they don't have a KU option, so the conversion rates will likely be in the 1:20 (for a brilliantly written description with proper copywriting… which isn't many of them) or 1:30 – 1:40 for 99.9% of the books.

This is because KU subscribers are getting "FREE" books when they see ads, so this DRAMATICALLY improves the conversion rate.

On B&N, this isn't an option, so the rate will ONLY be people who are willing to BUY. That's important to remember.

If the CTR is 3%, which is WILDLY optimistic AND the author was buying 1 million impressions (because they have piles of cash lying around), they would likely get 1 sale for every $7.00 spent.

Conversion rate of 1:30.

CTR of 3%.

3% of 1,000 is 30.

Hence, one sale per 1,000 impressions.

A more reasonable CTR is 1.5%, so 1 sale for every $14.00 spent. (See above math and double, because now they're only getting 15 clicks per 1,000.)

Few folks have the depth of series to pull off those numbers profitably.

Of course, for the authors that only buy, say, 100,000 impressions, they will spend $110 and likely get (assuming 1.5% CTR) 5 sales.

The math doesn't work.

Now this is NOT to say it can't be done profitably.

Who are the authors that could make money at these rates?

Those with long series!

If you're wide AND you have 12 books in your series AND they are priced at full-price (I consider that to be $4.99)…

AND you've got a description with proper copywriting…

…then your chances at profitable ROI are reasonable—possibly even good.

If you've got 5 books priced at $2.99, and your description is a synopsis of what's in the book, you'll fail.

So, consider carefully the math (sorry I had to use that word, even though I know it makes you want to throw a wet cat at my face).

This has been a public service announcement from Math… the misunderstood but wildly sexy word that is grotesquely underappreciated.

Sincerely,

Math

P.S. I'm really nice if you just get to know me.

CHAPTER SIXTY-ONE

Description Thirty-Nine: Christian Historical

Author: Chris Lambert
Title: *Brother James*
Price: $3.99
Genre: Christian Historical Fiction

Before:

When your parents know, but you don't.

James is growing up in the first century, although he doesn't realize it. The brutal Romans occupy the Promised Land, the Pharisees think just about everything is a sin, and the bandits are trying to start a rebellion. And everyone thinks the Saviour will show up any time now to overthrow the Romans. There's something else James doesn't know - his very own brother is growing up to be the Promised Messiah.

Analysis:

The big negative that jumped out at me was the use of "think" twice. At this point, I don't think I need to mention the giant block of text, because I've covered the evils of giant blocks of texts many times, and to continue to write "giant block of text" would be echoing, which is annoying, so I'll assume you now cringe whenever you see a giant block of text, and I just won't even bring it up.

Meeks Version:

In the occupied Promise Land…

…everything is a sin.

Where is their Savior?

James, growing up in the first century, is surrounded by chaos. Surviving can be a challenge. But there is something special about his brother, and he had no idea what is coming next.

Bandits begin to start a rebellion.

The Pharisees want to stop it.

The Romans are brutal to all who oppose them.

Who will win?

You'll adore this brilliantly researched, fictional account of James's life. Both devout and non-religious readers agree that this is a finely crafted story that will keep you enthralled, because Ms. Lambert is a gifted writer.

Get it now.

Analysis:

You'll notice that throughout this book, I've stuck to a theme with the descriptions: the hook, a short paragraph, a couple more hooks, maybe another paragraph, then bring the reader in with a "You'll…because" and a call-to-action.

When I brought the reader in, I put the "because" in a second sentence. I wanted to get in one more plug to try to broaden the audience beyond only the deeply religious, as the reviews indicated that some non-devout folks had enjoyed it, too.

CHAPTER SIXTY-TWO

DESCRIPTION FORTY - THRILLER

Author: Brian Meeks
Title: *A Touch to Die For*
Price: $4.99
Genre: Thriller

Before:

Praise for A Touch To Die For:

"I could hardly put the story down."
"The plot is too brilliant to even try to relate and the characters, unique. Worth the read."
"Loved the characters and story line."

Mitch had no idea he was being watched.

For decades Paul couldn't let it go. The personal slight pecked at his brain just before the quiet of sleep arrived. It fueled the hate. His money, success, and the fame almost got him past it until he saw his nemesis Mitch with that beautiful woman.

Mitch couldn't believe he was finally with her. A lifetime of distant longing faded and turned into joy. The scales of happiness seemed tipped in his favor. Nothing could ruin his day.

He was wrong.

Paul knew that killing Mitch wouldn't satiate his lust for vengeance. He needed more. It had to be devastating to the core and last for the rest of Mitch's life. He would make Mitch a murder. Better yet, he would make the world believe that their beloved author was a deranged serial killer.

Who will win?

Who will survive?

You won't believe the twists and turns in this suspense thriller.

Pick up your copy with just one click.

How did you decide to dip your toes into the suspense and thriller genre?

I had just finished the fourth book in my *Henry Wood Detective* mystery series and was ready to begin a new novel. The problem was I didn't know yet what book 5 in the series would be about. When I shop for something to read I love looking for suspense thrillers and mystery bestsellers and decided that a psychological thriller might be fun to write.

Where did you get the idea for your first thriller kindle book?

The books I enjoy in the thriller genre always make me ask a question. In *A Touch To Die For*, I wanted to explore what it might be like for a genius to evolve into a serial killer. All the serial killers I can remember are geniuses who seem to know every detail about how to get away with murder. Surely there must have been a learning curve?

Analysis:

This was one of the first descriptions I wrote after studying copywriting. Sadly, I didn't save the original, which I recall was pretty bad.

The problem here is it's still way too much synopsis. And I've changed my position on the crap at the bottom.

The original point was that it allowed me to do SEO for Amazon by stuffing in some keywords. Yes, that is a valid reason, but alas, my book doesn't do well in organic search even with this, so I feel it's more negative than positive.

I'm taking it out to create a lighter description.

Meeks (New) Version:

She looked beautiful at dinner.

He had longed for her…

Someone was watching… filled with rage.

In a hotel, with the sheets still warm, Mitch looked at her. It seemed like a lifetime of desire that had only led to friendship…until last night. Now he had to clear his head. Could he avoid screwing up? Getting past the "friend zone" was one thing, but what he really wanted was love.

He told her he had to leave.

But he would be back.

She seemed pleased at the thought.

Mitch left for the airport. He had never been happier. Years of distant longing faded into joy. Nothing can ruin it for me, he thought.

He was wrong.

Paul carried with him the pain of a single slight in college. It fueled him, and the hatred drove his success. Now a billionaire, he had almost put the memory behind him… until he saw them together. In an instant, he had the perfect plan… but how does one become a serial killer and pin it on someone else?

He would need to be careful.

It would take planning.

Could he ruin Mitch's life in the most horrible way possible and walk away?

You'll love this thriller, because it's a game of cat and mouse.

Get it now.

Analysis:

There's a lot less about the plot and much more hooks. I kept a little bit from the one above—the "He was wrong" line was solid. This is a much better description.

It should be noted, as this is important for all of you reading, it is MUCH harder to work on one's own descriptions than others. I've written hundreds of descriptions for others.

Though it was easier today than it was two years ago when I did the first post-copywriting study, it still took me twice as long as normal.

We are too close to our stories.

If you want to get good at this copywriting stuff, help other authors with their descriptions when they ask for it. The practice will make working on your own easier, but it will always be tough NOT to include too much of the good juicy stuff you're excited to talk about.

INTERESTING DATA: This is NOT scientific, but it is interesting.

A Touch to Die For is a stand-alone book that I use only for research, which means I do not advertise it unless I'm specifically trying something new. As of the writing of this book, it has NOT been advertised in the last 90 days.

Nineteen days ago, I wrote the version above and made the change. Let's look at the numbers, which I must say could be nothing more than random luck, but they're still interesting and come entirely from organic traffic.

Before = 71 days
After = 19

Before sales = 1 for an average of .014 sales per day
After sales = 1 for an average of .052 per day.

Okay, that's a great example of data that isn't really worth too much, because it's clear that this book periodically gets a sale, and in another 52 days, it may not get any more and will be just the same.

This is important to remember when analyzing your own books. Too little data can lead to wrong conclusions.

But wait... there's more...

We have some other data, too: the page reads, which are better because of their granularity. Let's look at them and see how they compare:

Before = 543
After = 921

That's quite a few more. But let's dig deeper. For 71 days *A Touch To Die For* averaged only 7.64 per day. But what's even more telling is the number of zero days, which was 58, compared to the after, which only had 1 zero day.

The after has averaged 48.47 pages per day. That's a 534% increase. And no matter what, even if there isn't a single page read that happens over the next 52 days, there will be MORE revenue after the change than before.

Again, and I admit this freely, the numbers are still statistically insignificant, but when I combine this data with all the times I've seen improvement from other authors, it seems reasonable to conclude that the new description has made an impact.

The important takeaway is that even if you are not doing any advertising, sometimes people organically find your book, and you still need to give it the best chance of being read possible.

Copywriting does that.

CHAPTER SIXTY-THREE

Dear author,

You made it to the end.

I'm proud of you. There was a lot of stuff to consider, and even with all of it, you'll need to practice to get good. But it's worth it.

So, what now?

1. Write your own description.
2. Join my Facebook group, Mastering Amazon Descriptions: An Author's Guide.
3. Leave a review. (You made it this far. Now let's see if you can manage a few words letting other authors know what you thought, for good or bad. You should be striving to do two things: get people to read your entire review, and paint me in such a light as to make the future Mrs. Brian Meeks, swoon. Is that too much to ask?
4. Go back and write your own post trying to get your author friends to buy this book. Use this link: books2read.com/u/47xrxa

Does it seem like I'm being a little selfish here? I mean, I already asked you to do that in the first chapter.

No.

Did you like the book?

Do you believe your new copywriting skills will help you succeed?

Would you like your author friends to sell more books, too?
For those who gave a triple "Yes," then why wouldn't you?

IMPORTANT: The reason I have a link you can use is that it's an affiliate link, which will allow me to track how many people get this far and do step 4.

You see, I do everything with an eye toward data. You're smack-dab in the middle of my back matter, and you didn't even know it.

Note: I realize that one is not supposed to use Affiliate Links in Kindle books, but I'm using the universal link creator from Draft2Digital so it should work.

Did the copywriting here cause you to take action?
I don't know.
But there may one day be a book where I write about my research into back matter. And you'll be helping.
There's a number 5 on the list, too:
5. Reread *Mastering Amazon Descriptions: An Author's Guide.*

Lastly, if you like my writing (and why wouldn't you? I'm freaking adorable) then you'll love my other non-fiction titles, the last three I wrote with Honoree Corder (except the book about the 1987 Iowa Hawkeyes Men's basketball season. You wouldn't like that one). Check them out. You'll learn more great stuff. (All of these are available on Amazon.)

- *Mastering Amazon Ads: An Author's Guide*
- *The Nifty 15: Write Your Book in Just 15 Minutes a Day! (The Prosperous Writer 2)*
- *The Prosperous Writer's Guide to Making More Money: Habits, Tactics, and Strategies for Making a Living as a Writer*
- *The Prosperous Writer's Guide to Finding Readers: Build Your Author Brand, Raise Your Profile, and Find Readers to Delight*

Now go slay some dragons. I know you're ready.

One last thing…

Can I be hired to write a description or three?

Yes. I charge **$100** per description or **$225** for three.

This is not something I intend to do for the rest of my life, but for a while, I'm open to writing some for authors who may find it helpful.

How do you hire me?

A more organized author would have a website set up, but you'll just have to find me on Facebook, friend me, and then send me a Direct Message (DM).

It's on a first-come, first-serve basis.

My hope, though, is most of you will do it yourselves, but for those who would like to start off with a "Meeks Description", then you're welcome to ask for my services.

Oh, and one more "one last thing":

I teach a freaking awesome course about ads, analysis, copywriting, back matter, and other stuff: Meeks Master Class — if you're reading the print version, type this into your browser bar:

https://meeks-master-classes.teachable.com/p/mastering-amazon-ads-an-author-s-course/

If you use the code (GuineaPigsRock) you'll save 30%.